Published by My Littl' Workshop
First Edition
Printed in the United States of America
Cover by Prince Jai

This work is a spiritual, artistic, and intellectual expression of the author's lived experiences and divine revelations. Any resemblance to real persons, living or dead, is purely coincidental unless otherwise stated.

For the seekers, the wounded, the bold, the holy, the rising.

May you always remember your power.

This Is Not a Book, This Is a Weapon: Sacred Writings for the Untouchable Soul

Dedication

I dedicate this to myself—

To the self that has been doing this soul work long before there were titles, applause, or recognition.
To the self who nearly forgot herself in service to others.

To the self who had to become her own rescue mission.
To the self who reached into the sacred toolkit to realign, to remember, to rise again.

I dedicate this to me, because rarely have I done so.

Because my power is real.
Because my path is sacred.
Because weaving souls back together is no easy feat.

This work is not performance—this is energy work,
And it can be the most rewarding, yet the most draining,

Because some take and forget to say thank you,
While others take, knowing, and still choose silence.

This is not written from ego,
But from a place of spiritual etiquette.

Learn to say thank you——

To your teachers, in front of them and behind them.
There's a blessing in the power of the tongue.

Speak it, and they will bless you wherever they are.

This journey you're on——it won't always be easy.
This isn't "trending healing."
This is deep, raw, soul-resurrecting work.
But here you are.
Doing it.

So I also dedicate this to you,
_____ (insert your name).
You are in for a ride.

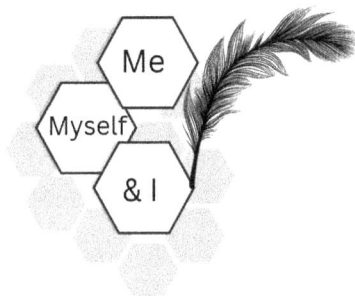

"I did not write this to impress you. I wrote this to awaken you. If you're brave enough to keep reading, you just might remember who you truly are."

—— Rev. Dr. Marie Brevil

I Am Becoming: The Self-Love Era — I'm Choosing Me
(former title)

A Personal Note from the Writer

From the depths of my soul to the depth of yours
—read this with intention.

This is not just a book.
This is a companion.

A calling.
A consecrated offering.

This is a homecoming to your truest self.

If this is your first time ever touching something
like this—
I honor your courage.

I see your trembling hands, your curious heart.
I invite you to let go of fear.
To breathe deeply and walk in anyway.

If your soul led you here, you're ready—
Even if your mind still trembles.

Let this be your new scripture, your new sacred
text.

Put it by your bedside.
Sleep with it close to your heart.

Return to it when you feel lost.
Return to it when you feel found.

No disrespect to the Bible or any sacred text—
But this too is sacred.

This too was born through Spirit.

This too came from a long line of those who walked before us,

Who whispered into my ears,
Who held my hands as I wrote,
Who channeled fire, truth, and medicine into every page.

Treat this with reverence.
Treat this like the inheritance you forgot you were promised.

Not because I wrote it—
But because it was written through me, for you.

This is not a one-time read.
This is a life-long walk.

A companion for the days you rise victorious
And the nights you collapse in silence.

Put your ego down.
Set your pride aside.
Stand in your nakedness——
And let these words wash over you like holy water.

Let them bruise you into freedom and bless you into clarity.

Refer back to this book in times of war and times of peace.

When you're being called to rise.
When you're being called to rest.

This is your sword and your sanctuary.

If you let it, this book will remind you who you are.

If you let it, this book will not just awaken you—
It will arm you.

You've been asking for signs.
You've been crying for healing.
You've been begging for answers.

This is one of them.
So don't play with it.

Honor it.
Use it.
But use it wisely.

With responsibility.
With power.
With deep love.

Because now that you hold this,
Much is required.

Walk with grace.
Walk with purpose.
And walk with the knowing that you are never alone.

May your journey with this book
be blessed, protected, and overflowing
with divine revelation.

With all reverence,

Rev. Dr. Marie Brevil
Your sister in power, healing, and unshakable truth

Note any aha moment

INTRODUCTION

Welcome to the Threshold

Dear Reader,

You did not arrive here by accident.
Something in you called this work forward——
a whisper, a pull, a knowing.

Maybe you were seeking healing, clarity, strength, or just a spark.

Maybe you weren't seeking at all,
but spirit brought you here anyway.

This is not your typical collection of affirmations.
This is not the sugar-coated inspiration the world is used to.

This is raw,
fierce,
soul-deep remembering.

This is sacred rage and holy peace.
This is ancient truth wrapped in modern flame.
This is transformation coded into language.

You may feel goosebumps.
You may feel seen.
You may feel disrupted——in the best way.

Because the words within these pages are not soft lullabies.
They are portals, mirrors, keys.

They may stir your blood and open your spirit.
They may challenge what you thought you knew.

But if you stay open—if you let them in—
they may also bring deliverance.
So take your time.
Breathe between each page.
Pause when your heart speaks up.

And trust that whatever is meant to reach you... will.

This is your journey now.
This is your soul on paper.

And we are honored to walk with you.

Let the unraveling begin.
Let the remembering begin.
Let the rising begin.

With fierce love and divine truth,
We welcome you.

– Your Divine Coach.

How to Use This Book

This is not just a book. It's a tool, a key, a spiritual weapon.
Read this not like you're flipping through pages—
but like you're unlocking parts of yourself.

This book is a mirror, a portal, a fire-starter.
You can move through it linearly or intuitively.
There is no right or wrong way—
only the way that speaks to your spirit.

Here are some ways you may work with this book:

As a Daily Ritual
Read one declaration, poem, or invocation each day.
Sit with it. Reflect. Speak it aloud.
Let it awaken your truth.
Let it stir your power.

As a Spiritual Cleanse
When energy feels heavy, flip to any page.
Ask the divine: "What do I need today?"
Trust where your hand lands.
Read that piece like a prayer, a reminder, a weapon.

As a Mirror for Healing
When you feel broken, betrayed, small, or unseen—
find yourself within these pages.
Let the words remind you that you are not your pain.
You are the healer. The fire. The storm and the stillness.

As a Writing or Reflection Tool

After reading, journal (you know, write):

- What was stirred within me?
- Where did I feel this in my body?
- What memory, voice, or ancestor echoed through this?
- Write as much or as little as you need.
- This book pairs well with your own voice.

As a Gateway to the Divine

Read the writings aloud, especially when you feel far from Spirit.

Speak with intention.
Call in your ancestors.
Claim your name.
These are not mere affirmations.
They are activations.

Guidance for Your Journey

- Be open. These words may challenge what you thought you knew. Let them.
- Be gentle. Not every piece is meant to feel soft. Some are here to cut away what no longer belongs.
- Be brave. Transformation is not easy. But you've already survived the hardest parts.
- Be sacred. Light a candle. Burn incense. Wear white. Sit by water. Invoke your guides. Make this journey holy.

Lastly,

This is not the kind of book you finish and shelve.
This is a living book.
Return to it often.

Let it grow with you.
Let it speak to the new version of you each time you rise.

May it become an altar.
May it become a weapon.
May it become a bridge between who you were
and who you are becoming.

Now that you know how to use this work...
go ahead and begin.

You are ready.

You've always been.

Note any aha moment

Introduction:

I Am Becoming: The Self-Love Era — I'm Choosing Me (former title). This is a book of positive messages and affirmations for your becoming: "This Is Not a Book, This Is a Weapon: Sacred Writings for the Untouchable Soul."

When everything feels like it's falling apart, when the weight of the world threatens your peace, when you're questioning who you are and where you're going—these words are your return.

Return to self.
Return to strength.
Return to truth.

These messages are not here to fix you. They are here to remind you that you were never broken.
That even in moments of darkness, there is still light within you.
That you do not need to keep fighting yourself over what has already passed.

Let this be your sacred space.
A place to breathe, affirm, and rise.

No matter how lost you feel, you can always come back home—to you.

Let's start with a beautiful affirmation for self-love:

"I am worthy of love, kindness, and respect. I honor my unique journey and embrace every part of myself with compassion and gratitude. Each day, I grow stronger in loving and accepting who I am."

There may be days when you question your reflection—when you forget how powerful, soft, divine, and worthy you truly are. In those moments, come back to this truth: self-love is not earned through perfection, it is reclaimed through presence.

You don't need to be anyone else. You don't need to copy a single soul. You are not too much. You are not too late. You are simply becoming.

Affirmation:

I am worthy of love, kindness, and respect.
I honor my unique journey and embrace every part of myself with compassion and gratitude.
Each day, I grow stronger in loving and accepting who I am.

Healing in My Own Time

There is no rush on your healing. No timeline to meet. No perfection to chase. You are not behind, and you are not broken. You are unfolding in the way that only you can—beautifully, deeply, and truly.

The need to be perfect is a weight you no longer have to carry. Let it go. Let softness in. Let time be your ally, not your enemy. Healing doesn't mean fixing—it means remembering your wholeness.

You are not here to impress the world by being perfect. You are here to heal, to grow, to bloom in your own time. Let go of the deadlines placed on your heart. The journey is not a race—it's a sacred unfolding. Your imperfections are not flaws; they are fingerprints of your humanity.

Be kind to yourself. Allow space for your becoming. There is power in patience and grace in taking your time. You are not behind—you are right where you need to be.

Affirmation:

I release the need to be perfect and allow myself to heal in my own time.
I trust in my inner strength, knowing I am whole, worthy, and enough just as I am.
With each breath, I welcome love, growth, and peace into my life.

The Radiance of Authenticity

There comes a time when you no longer look sideways. A time when you stop comparing, stop shrinking, stop waiting for applause that may never come. This is that time. This is your self-love era.

A season of truth, beauty, and unshakable confidence. Let them pretend not to see. Let them stay silent. Their silence is not your signal to stop shining—it's confirmation that your light is loud. You were never meant to blend in. You were meant to bloom boldly. This is your time. Don't apologize for it. Don't soften your power. Just keep becoming.

Affirmation:

I am fully immersed in my self-love era, radiating beauty, confidence, and divine feminine energy.
I don't need to copy anyone—I am my own muse, my own masterpiece.

While others may watch in silence, pretending not to see, I refuse to dim my light.

I stay true to myself, authentic and unwavering.
My glow is not for validation but for my own joy.
I keep rising, loving, and embracing all that I am. I am enough, I am divine, I am unstoppable.

The Devotion of Self-Love

Self-love is not a fleeting moment——it's a lifelong commitment. It's not just about feeling good in the moment, but about showing up for yourself every single day. Gratitude isn't a temporary goal; it's a way of being.

No matter what life throws at me, I choose to remain in gratitude, because my worth is not defined by circumstances but by how I honor myself. Self-love is getting up even when I'm tired, pushing forward when my soul needs strength. But it's also knowing when to rest, when to breathe, when to listen to my body's wisdom.

It's the discernment to recognize the difference between true self-love and self-lies——between pushing through for growth and burning out for validation. I choose consistency. I choose gratitude. I choose real, deep, unwavering self-love.

Affirmation:

I honor myself with devotion and care.
Each day, I rise with intention and rest with compassion.
I trust my body's wisdom and my soul's rhythm.
I no longer perform love——I embody it.
My self-love is sacred, strong, and sustainable.
In all things, I choose what nourishes me deeply.

When the Light Returns

Even when everything feels dark, I choose to speak life into myself. I remind my soul that life is still worth living. I smile —not because everything is perfect, but because I still have light within me. I get up, I show up—for me. I bathe in love, I anoint myself with care. I put on perfume, lotion, and essential oils—not just to smell good, but to feel good. I deserve to feel soft, sacred, and whole.

I am not just the depressed version of me—I am evolving, unfolding, becoming. I allow myself to see beauty again. I allow myself to believe in more. I am still here, and that means something. I am worthy of care, of love, of joy. Today, I choose me.

Affirmation:

I am allowed to be soft in my strength and whole in my healing.
Even in darkness, my spirit glows.
I am not broken—I am blooming through the cracks.
I treat myself with tenderness, grace, and intention.
Today, I rise in my own light and reclaim my joy.
I choose life, I choose beauty, I choose me.

The Sound of My Own Peace

Even when the voices in my head won't let me rest, I choose to speak peace over my mind. I am not my thoughts——I am the one who listens, the one who chooses. When the past rises, I remind myself: I survived it. I am here. I am healing. I don't have to run from what hurt me, because I am not there anymore.

I honor my past, but I do not live in it. I choose presence. I choose peace. I breathe deeply and anchor myself in this moment. I deserve peace. I deserve freedom. I am not broken——I am becoming whole. And even when the noise is loud, my soul knows silence, and my spirit knows strength. I return to myself. I am safe here.

Affirmation:

I am not the chaos in my mind——I am the calm in my breath.
I choose peace even when fear whispers.
I honor my healing, not my hurt.
Every thought does not define me.
I choose which ones to keep, and today I choose grace.
I return to my center.
I am rooted, I am whole, I am free.

Built for This Moment

Remind yourself today: you are a wonderful person. You are amazing—yes, even in the middle of what you're facing. Life is not over. Take heart. Shake it off. There is still hope. You will be fine. Breathe, and take it one day at a time. You can handle anything—no world problem, no sacrifice, no setback can shut you down.

You were built for this. You can handle fame, you can handle money, you can handle prosperity—because you're rooted in something real. Stay connected with your purpose. Let your heart lead. Whatever sacrifice is needed, you have it in you. Your heart is that big. Nothing is bigger than you. You've come too far to stop now. So keep rising. Keep believing. Keep going. You got this.

Affirmation:

I am divinely equipped to overcome, evolve, and expand.
Even when pressure surrounds me, I rise rooted in truth.
I am steady, unshaken, and guided by purpose.
Every challenge is a stepping stone to my greatness.
I don't shrink—I soar. I don't fear—I flow.
Today, I remember who I am: powerful, purposeful, and prepared.

You Are Enough, Now and Always

Know this——you are enough. Not tomorrow, not when you accomplish more, not when others say so. Right now, just as you are. And so it is. Never buy into the lie that you need approval to be worthy.

Your worth is not up for debate. You are amazing. You are a gift to this world. Your presence matters. Your light matters. Remember that. Breathe it in. Let it settle in your bones. You are enough. Always have been. Always will be.

Affirmation:

I am enough, exactly as I am.
My worth is inherent, unshaken by opinions or outcomes.
I do not chase validation——
I embody truth.
I radiate light simply by being.
I honor who I am today, without needing to prove or perform.
I am a divine creation, whole and worthy in every breath I take.

Anchored in Source, Aligned with Purpose

Your entire life is about your God——your Source, your Truth. Don't get distracted by the noise of the world or the weight of its problems. Stay focused. Stay in alignment. Keep your heart anchored in honor and your spirit rooted in purpose.

You are already popular in your own world, already chosen, already seen. You don't need the world's approval when you walk with divine connection. You can handle anything—— because God is with you, within you, and ahead of you. You are guided, protected, and empowered. Stay faithful. Stay ready. You were made for this."

Affirmation:

I walk with divine purpose, and I am aligned with truth.
The approval of the world cannot replace my connection to Source.
I am already seen, already known, already chosen.
God goes before me, surrounds me, and dwells within me.
I do not fear——I stay focused, faithful, and firm in my calling.
I was made for this moment, and I rise with strength, clarity, and grace.

Walking with Purpose Until the Return

When the time comes, you'll return to the arms of your Grand Architect. But until then—live fully. Do the sacred work your soul was sent here to accomplish. Don't let distractions steal your focus. No illness, struggle, or storm can stop the divine purpose placed within you. Stay in prayer, stay affirmed, stay deeply rooted.

Speak life over yourself, even in silence. Keep yourself prayed up, joyful, and centered. Don't miss out on becoming all you were made to be. Don't let mistakes or misunderstandings steer you off course. You are here for a reason—divinely designed and heaven-backed. Walk boldly with honor. Keep moving forward.

Affirmation:

I am divinely guided and protected on my journey.
My purpose is strong, and no obstacle can stop me.
I remain rooted in prayer, joy, and faith.
Every step I take is in alignment with my sacred assignment.
I am here for a reason, and I honor that truth daily.
I walk with confidence and grace until I return to my Grand Architect.

Rise in Your Divine Power

Activate the immense power within your soul—because you are a superpower in human form. Even when life feels like it's pressing you down again and again, remember your spirit is built for resurrection. You don't stay down; you always rise.

Each time you get up to pray, to speak life over yourself, you cleanse and realign your energy. Doubt has no hold on you because you are being refined, not defeated. Reclaim your focus, your light, and your divine purpose. You were made for greatness. Walk boldly in that truth every day.

Affirmation:

I am a divine superpower, built to rise and overcome.
Each challenge refines me, making me stronger and brighter.
I cleanse my mind and spirit of doubt and fear.
I reclaim my focus and walk fully aligned with my purpose.
I am power. I am purpose. I am divine.
I walk boldly, knowing who I am.

Reprogram and Rise

You have the sacred power to reprogram your mind and spirit. Affirm your life and your purpose daily. Own your divine right to exist and thrive. Transition upward into greater visions, bigger achievements, and a broader impact. Grow wide and tall—expand your energy and let your light shine louder than ever before.

Make space within yourself for more love, peace, and success. Remember, you are blessed and carry a deep, abiding bliss. Each day, you step more fully into your power as a gift to this world and any realm you enter. Feel your greatness and claim it fully.

Affirmation:

I reprogram my mind and soul for growth and greatness.
I affirm my life, purpose, and divine right to be here.
I transition upward into bigger dreams and wider impact.
My light shines brighter and louder every day.
I make room for more love, peace, and success in my life.
I am blessed, I am blissful, and I am a gift to this world.
I feel amazing, and I own my power.

Beyond Limits, Within Grace

You stand on a higher plane that those who are unaligned cannot fathom. There is no need to shrink or dim your light —you are vast, powerful, and destined for greatness. Your God hears you, watches over you, and constantly provides. You are cherished and favored beyond measure. Darkness cannot linger where your light shines; truth and power surround you.

Gratitude is your key, unlocking doors to blessings and opportunities beyond your imagination. You are capable, unstoppable, and victorious. Remember this truth every day —you already carry the victory within you.

Affirmation:

I stand on a higher level, unshaken by those who cannot understand my light.
My God listens and provides abundantly.
I am special, favored, and never forgotten.
Darkness has no place in my life—only light, truth, and power prevail.
I am grateful, and gratitude opens doors beyond my dreams.
I am able, limitless, and always victorious.
I carry the victory within me now.

Guarding My Light, Embracing My Purpose

Your energy is sacred, and you hold the power to protect it fiercely. Darkness and negativity have no place in your life because you were born from the light—pure, resilient, and destined to shine.

Healing is a journey, and you honor that process by staying centered and full in yourself. Being single is not a setback; it is a sacred space for growth and clarity, far better than allowing toxic energies to disrupt your peace.

Your purpose is divine and your path is clear. You walk confidently, immune to distractions, and aligned with your prosperity. Your light is your shield, and it will guide you always.

Affirmation:

I release all bad energy and protect my soul fiercely.
I am born of light, growing stronger and brighter every day.
Being single is my time to heal and center myself fully.
I refuse to carry the weight of negativity or destructive karmas.
My purpose is divine, my plan is for prosperity, and I stay focused on my path.
I walk in my light, unshaken and true to myself.

Aligned and Unshakable

When your soul is aligned, your path becomes clear and your focus sharpens. You are destined for greatness, and nothing or no one should steer you away from your true purpose.

Trust your inner guidance and be your own oracle—discern what serves your growth and what does not. False voices may try to pull you off course, but your strength and clarity will keep you grounded. Protect your energy by staying purpose-driven and unwavering. Your journey is unique, and it deserves your full commitment.

Affirmation:

My soul is aligned with my highest purpose.
I remain focused on my dreams and plans.
I refuse to be distracted or dragged into what is not mine.
I stand strong for myself and the divine within me.
I am my own oracle, listening only to my truth.
I stay fully occupied with purposeful action and remain steadfast on my path.

Awake and Empowered

In a world full of confusion and distraction, staying awake and conscious is a radical act of self-love and resistance. You are not here to be controlled or diminished by fear or illusion. When discouragement tries to pull you down, reconnect with your strength and the grounding power of nature.

Walk barefoot, breathe deeply, and remind yourself that challenges are temporary. Your decisions shape your future —choose wisely with clarity and courage. You were made to rise above, to shine, and to thrive.

Affirmation:

I choose to stay awake and conscious.
I refuse to be enslaved by fear or illusion.
When I feel discouraged, I ground myself in nature and breath.
I make decisions from strength, not fear.
Temporary challenges do not define my permanent path.
I am made to rise, to shine, and to thrive.

Strength Beyond the Storm

When sadness feels heavy and the way forward seems unclear, remember that your life is much bigger than any moment of pain. You carry within you a strength and wisdom that no hardship can diminish.

The world may try to weigh you down, but your spirit is built to rise. Keep sowing light, keep doing good, and hold your focus steady. Let negativity bounce back to where it came from, while you stay pure, aligned, and unshaken in your purpose.

Affirmation:

I am bigger than my struggles.
I am stronger and wiser than my challenges.
No sadness can hold me down forever.
I sow light and goodness every day.
Negative energy returns to its sender.
I remain focused, pure, and aligned.
I do not give up—I keep moving forward.

Strength in the Storm

Even in moments of weakness or chaos, your strength is real and returning. Clarity is unfolding, guiding you gently back to your true path.

Confusion has no power over you because you are anchored in purpose and truth. Trust each step—especially the uncertain ones—as part of your divine journey. You are present, purposeful, and moving forward with grace and peace.

Affirmation:

I am strong, even when I feel weak.
Clarity comes to me in every moment.
I am not lost; I am being redirected.
Confusion holds no power over me.
I walk in light and speak my truth.
I breathe in calm and release all fear.
I am anchored in my divine purpose.
Today, I move with grace, power, and peace."

I Am Safe in My Becoming

Even when the voices in my head won't let me rest, I choose to speak peace over my mind. I am not my thoughts——I am the one who listens, the one who chooses. When the past rises, I remind myself: I survived it. I am here. I am healing. I don't have to run from what hurt me, because I am not there anymore. I honor my past, but I do not live in it. I choose presence. I choose peace.

I breathe deeply and anchor myself in this moment. I deserve peace. I deserve freedom. I am not broken——I am becoming whole. And even when the noise is loud, my soul knows silence, and my spirit knows strength. I return to myself. I am safe here.

Affirmation:

I am not trapped by my past——I am transformed by my healing.
Every breath I take is a return to calm.
I release the noise and honor the silence within me.
Peace is not outside me——it lives in my spirit.
I choose now. I choose me. I choose serenity.
I am the calm after every storm.

(Same message as "The Sound of My Own Peace" but different affirmations)

Embrace Your Authentic Power

Your true strength comes from being unapologetically yourself. You don't need to imitate or compare—your unique light is what makes you shine. Authenticity is a rare and powerful gift.

When you embrace who you really are, you unlock doors to joy, freedom, and success that no copycat ever could. Celebrate your individuality; it's your superpower that no one else can replicate.

Affirmations:

I am perfectly and powerfully me.
My authenticity is my greatest strength.
I release the need to fit in or imitate.
Being myself attracts the right people and opportunities.
I honor my unique journey and celebrate my individuality.
I trust my voice and value my perspective.
I am a one-of-a-kind masterpiece, and that is enough.
My authenticity lights the way for others to do the same.

Living in Gratitude and Consistency

Gratitude is not just a feeling; it's a way of life that transforms every moment into a blessing. When you make gratitude your lifestyle, you create a foundation of positivity and abundance that uplifts your spirit daily.

Consistency is the loving commitment you make to yourself —showing up, nurturing your growth, and honoring your journey no matter what. Together, gratitude and consistency form a powerful love language you speak to yourself, reinforcing your worth and fueling your progress.

Affirmations:

Gratitude fills my heart and shapes my reality.
I consistently choose to honor and love myself.
Every day, I cultivate thankfulness for all I am and all I have.
Consistency is my promise to myself, and I keep it with joy.
I attract more blessings by appreciating what is already mine.
My steady actions reflect my deep self-respect.
I am patient and gentle with myself as I grow.
Gratitude and consistency empower my healing and success.

Shining Through the Darkness

Even when life feels dark or uncertain, your light is never truly dimmed. Showing up for yourself is a radical act of self-love and resilience. Dressing yourself with care, anointing your spirit with intention, and stepping into your day are declarations that you matter—especially to yourself.

This sacred ritual nurtures your soul, reminding you that your worth and radiance are constant, regardless of circumstances. You are your own sanctuary, and you choose to honor that light every day.

Affirmations:

I am a beacon of light, even in my darkest moments.
I honor myself through care, ritual, and presence.
Dressing for me is an act of love and empowerment.
I nurture my spirit with every anointing and intention.
My inner light shines brighter with every choice I make for myself.
I show up fully for my own healing and joy.
Darkness cannot extinguish the fire within me.
I am worthy of care, celebration, and sacred attention.
Each day, I rise and radiate my authentic glow.

Choosing Peace Beyond the Past

Though my past may echo in my mind like a shadow, I refuse to be imprisoned by its weight. I acknowledge the memories, the lessons, and the scars, but I do not let them define my present or dictate my future. I am more than what I've been through—I am who I am becoming.

Each day, I reclaim my power by choosing peace, healing, and freedom. I am the author of my story, and I write it with courage, grace, and hope. Peace is my path forward, and I walk it with steady steps.

Affirmations:

I honor my past but I do not live in it.
I release what no longer serves my highest good.
Peace fills my mind, body, and soul.
I am free from the chains of old wounds.
My past shapes me but does not limit me.
I am healing with every breath I take.
I choose calm over chaos, love over fear.
I am safe, whole, and at peace right now.
I forgive myself and others, freeing my spirit.
Each day, I grow stronger in my peace and power.

Note any aha moment

Built for Greatness

I am a wonderful person——radiant, resilient, and full of potential. No burden, no setback, no challenge is heavy enough to shut me down or dim my light. Every experience has shaped me, strengthened me, and prepared me to rise higher.

Greatness is not just a dream; it is my birthright and my destiny. I stand tall with confidence, knowing that I am capable of incredible things. I was built for greatness, and nothing can stop my ascent.

Affirmations:

I am worthy of all the good life offers.
Challenges only fuel my determination.
My strength grows with every trial I overcome.
I radiate confidence and positivity.
I am unstoppable, courageous, and bold.
I attract opportunities that align with my greatness.
I am a beacon of hope and inspiration to others.
My potential is limitless and expanding every day.
I embrace my power and walk my path with purpose.
I was born to shine and to succeed.

Soul Freedom Declaration

This is more than a release—this is a holy reclamation. I renounce sadness, discouragement, and every energy that was never mine to carry. I declare the breakage of every ungodly soul tie, every unhealthy attachment, every spiritual hook that kept me bound in cycles of pain.

I no longer agree with trauma bonds or energetic contracts formed in fear, confusion, or manipulation. I call upon Infinite Intelligence to take over. I call in the presence of my wise and loving ancestors to support me now. I reclaim my soul. I reclaim my body.

I reclaim my mind. I free myself and anyone else bound by these cords. This chapter will not repeat. I trust my inner power. I honor my divine authority to sever what does not serve. I cut communication. I cut ties. I cut the connection, forever. And so it is.

Affirmations:

I am free from all ungodly ties—spiritually, emotionally, and mentally.
I revoke any unspoken contracts of pain and suffering.
I call back all parts of my power that were scattered in the past.

I am shielded by divine intelligence and ancestral wisdom.

I walk forward unchained, unburdened, and fully whole.

I release all false friendships and silent sabotage from my sphere.

I am no longer accessible to toxic communication or manipulation.

My spirit is sovereign. My peace is protected.

I walk in spiritual integrity and alignment.

I am free. I am clear. I am chosen to rise.

The Sacred Reclamation

I no longer participate in cycles of pain dressed as love. I no longer carry the weight of relationships that robbed me of clarity.

Every ungodly soul tie, every karmic loop, every unhealthy spiritual agreement—I now break. I dissolve the energy of any friendship, partnership, or connection formed through deception or control.

I speak freedom into my lineage. I speak release over my life. I am not here to live bound. I am here to live whole. With the help of divine presence and the ancestors who stand with me, I reclaim my light.

I trust that who I am becoming is too great to remain attached to what has expired. I forgive. I release. I rise.

Affirmations:

I am no longer tethered to people or pain that delay my purpose.
I call on Divine Power to break all soul contracts that keep me small.
I dissolve every cord tied through manipulation, guilt, or fear.

I reclaim my energy and restore my essence.

My ancestors surround me with truth and strength.

I release the need to explain my healing to those who misused me.

I am spiritually protected, emotionally balanced, and mentally clear.

I walk away without shame or regret.

I honor my healing by staying disconnected from harm.

I free myself, and in doing so, I bless others to heal too.

Break and Rise

I break every spiritual agreement not aligned with love, with peace, with the truth of who I am. I sever all ties made in confusion, loneliness, or desperation. Every soul connection meant to deceive or distract—be gone.

I call on Infinite Intelligence, I call on Divine Wisdom, I call on my benevolent ancestors—stand with me now. Oversee this breaking, and seal my freedom in light. I renounce sadness. I renounce the shame. I renounce the voices that made me doubt my strength. I take back what is mine—my voice, my body, my path.

I no longer seek closure through contact. I no longer engage what I've outgrown. I free me. I free them. May this cycle never return.

Affirmations:

I am no longer a home for pain, manipulation, or spiritual confusion.
I walk in sacred freedom and personal truth.
I cut all cords that drain my light or distort my vision.
I invite Divine Presence to fill every space that is now empty.
I reclaim my joy, my clarity, and my connection to Spirit.
I am not obligated to carry old energies into my new life.

I trust my intuition to lead me away from danger and toward peace.

I was never meant to live entangled in trauma—I was made to thrive.

I release all unhealthy emotional contracts, spoken or unspoken.

I am safe. I am sovereign. I am renewed.

No More Agreements with Pain

Today, I choose to be unavailable for anything rooted in harm. I no longer keep quiet to maintain peace that costs me my voice. I renounce every silent agreement I made with pain. I revoke access. I revoke consent.

Every tie built on guilt, shame, control, or codependency—I cut them all. I speak my name back into power. I am not obligated to serve anyone else's unhealed wounds. I stand with my ancestors as witnesses to my release. They walked so I could rise. And I honor them by not returning to what broke me. I am the one who breaks the cycle. I am the one who heals the lineage. I am the one who chooses freedom —again and again.

Affirmations:

I revoke every agreement I made in survival that now blocks my peace.
I am not required to carry anyone else's pain.
I cut emotional, mental, and spiritual cords tied through manipulation.
I am allowed to walk away without explaining my worth.
My healing is not up for debate or negotiation.
I am held by Divine Intelligence and ancestral protection.
I am not a dumping ground for anyone's karma.
I choose relationships that honor my light, not drain it.
I protect my peace like a sacred altar.
I am no longer bound. I am blessed and becoming

Closure Comes from Within

I do not need their apology to be free. I do not need their validation to heal. I carry the power of Divine Intelligence within me, and that is enough. Every time I chose silence over retaliation, every time I chose peace over chaos—I was sowing freedom.

I no longer wait for the closure of others to reclaim my energy. I create it. I command it. I consecrate it. With the ancestors watching, I speak life into my release.

May every karmic lesson now be complete. I am no longer bound by history. I am called into destiny.

Affirmations:

Closure does not come from them—it comes from the truth I claim.
I do not return to places that fractured my spirit.
I sever ties with dignity and divine clarity.
My energy is reserved for people and paths that nurture my soul.
I am not broken—I am reborn.
I no longer chase healing in the hands of those who hurt me.
I choose peace over familiarity.
I let go so that I can grow.
My freedom is not conditional—it is complete.
I forgive, I release, and I move forward.

Full Soul Sovereignty

I stand in the fullness of who I am. No counterfeit connection, no soul trap, no toxic communication has the right to my light. I cut ties—verbal, energetic, emotional, psychic. I do not look back. I do not return to what I had to heal from.

I call upon the Infinite, the Divine, the Ancestors, the Earth beneath me—to ground this freedom. I declare that I am whole without needing to fill my spirit with anyone else's chaos.

I trust my discernment. I trust my gifts. I trust my boundaries. I am spiritually clear, emotionally balanced, and mentally guarded by truth. This is my reset. This is my rise.

Affirmations:

I declare full sovereignty over my soul, body, and spirit.
I do not revisit places that violated my peace.
I cut ties from false love and fear-based connections.
I am protected by the divine blueprint of my purpose.
I refuse to carry guilt for choosing myself.
I honor the boundaries that my healing requires.
I am no longer entangled—I am elevated.
I do not need to feel guilty for walking away.
I protect my energy as sacred currency.
I am whole. I am healed. I am home within myself.

Final Invocation: Divine Completion and Soul Freedom

This is the hour of release.
This is the moment of sacred return.
I call my spirit back from every place it was scattered.
I gather myself in truth, in light, in full alignment.

I speak now, not just for me, but for all versions of me——
the wounded, the silenced, the surviving, the awakening.
We are one.
We are whole.
We are free.

By the authority of Infinite Intelligence, I now break:
every ungodly soul tie,
every toxic friendship and emotional entanglement,
every spiritual chain wrapped in disguise,
every karmic loop,
every ancestral agreement that no longer serves the light.
I declare it dissolved.

I reclaim what was stolen.
I recover what was forgotten.
I restore what was buried.
I redeem what was misused.

I call forth the strength of my ancestors,
the wisdom of my lineage,
and the breath of divine truth
to sanctify this breakage as sacred healing.
And now——I am free.

Closing Affirmations:

I reclaim my spirit, my body, my soul, my mind.
I break and dissolve every tie that does not serve my highest good.
I call on divine intelligence to reset my path and cleanse my timeline.
I am no longer bound by trauma, history, or unhealthy attachments.
My freedom is sealed by truth, protected by love, and confirmed by light.
I do not carry the weight of others. I release them in grace.
I walk forward with clarity, dignity, and divine direction.
I am whole again. I am strong again. I am me—fully, freely, and forever.

Take a break and take journal your experience so far.

Take a break and take journal your experience so far.

Soul-Tie Release Ritual (Optional Sacred Action)

What You'll Need:

- A quiet space (indoor or outdoor)
- A candle (white or black for purification)
- A bowl of water or a small fire-safe container
- A piece of paper and pen
- Grounding item (crystal, stone, or barefoot contact with earth)

Steps:

1. Prepare the Space:
2. Cleanse the area with incense, sound, or intention.
3. Light the candle. Call in divine presence: your God, ancestors, angels, Infinite Intelligence.
4. Write It Down:
5. On the paper, list the names, memories, or feelings tied to the soul ties, attachments, or toxic bonds you are ready to release.
6. Speak the Invocation (or read from the final message):
7. Read aloud the soul release invocation and affirmations with confidence and sacred authority.
8. Symbolic Breakage:
9. Burn the paper in a safe bowl or submerge it in water. As it dissolves, declare:
10. "This tie is broken. I am free. I am reclaimed."
11. Feel the shift as you say it.
12. Seal It:
13. Touch the earth (or your grounding item) and say:
14. "I return to myself. I walk in light. It is done."
15. Sit in stillness. Breathe. Feel your power restored.

Renouncing the Spirit of Discouragement & Breaking the Tie

I no longer carry the weight of sadness that was never mine to hold. Discouragement will not have dominion over my day, my destiny, or my divine design.

Today, I cut all cords tied to depression, spiritual heaviness, emotional deception, and energetic depletion. I am not bound by past wounds or by those who masked their harm in friendship.

I call on Infinite Intelligence. I call on Divine Order. I call on my Ancestors. Take over. Take control. Guide me. Reclaim me. I declare my soul sovereign.

I dissolve all ungodly soul ties, spiritual attachments, and karmic assignments sent to derail my purpose. I free myself and anyone connected to my pain. I seal this chapter with truth, with love, and with finality.

Affirmations:

I reclaim my spirit. I reclaim my mind. I reclaim my body.

I renounce sadness. I renounce discouragement. I renounce every lie that said I wasn't worthy of joy.

I am divinely protected and spiritually untouchable.

Every ungodly soul tie is broken. Every toxic attachment is dissolved.

I release people who were never meant to stay.
I cut the cords. I cease the contact.
I let them go completely and I do not return.

I am whole. I am healed. I am holy.
I walk away with power. I stay away with purpose.

Reclaiming Your Divine Blueprint

No soul tie, no trauma bond, no disguised deception can keep me from my freedom. I am not chained to sorrow. I do not worship pain. I release the need to suffer to feel seen. I walk away from every ungodly tie——whether emotional, sexual, spiritual, or ancestral——that tried to define me by wounds instead of wisdom.

I choose myself. I choose my healing. I call back my power from every place it was scattered. I speak peace over my nervous system. I let go of every word curse, every bitter root, every contract I never consented to. I break it now.

Affirmations:

I am no longer bound to old agreements that harmed me.
I cancel every spiritual contract made in ignorance or under distress.
I reclaim the blueprint of my soul——whole, divine, and free.
I trust my ability to break every chain.
I forgive myself and I free myself.
I choose sacred solitude over destructive company.
I am connected only to that which is aligned, blessed, and divinely assigned.
I move forward in peace, power, and purity.

Severing Ties & Standing in Wholeness

I do not belong to the past. I am not owned by the ones who tried to control my light. I was never meant to stay small to keep others comfortable. I declare my sovereignty in this moment.

I sever the ties——seen and unseen——that keep trying to pull me back into cycles I've outgrown. Friendships with hidden harm, relationships that drain me, old connections with secret motives——they are all undone. May all toxic ties return to the void. I walk in clarity. I walk in divine intelligence. I do not turn back. I do not relive this. I am delivered.

Affirmations:

I revoke permission for anyone to manipulate, drain, or tether me.
I am free from spiritual confusion and emotional chaos.
I see clearly. I choose wisely.
I no longer answer calls from my past. I pick up for my purpose.
My spirit is shielded. My energy is protected. My path is clear.
I no longer feel guilty for saving myself.
I was never meant to be trapped——I was born to be free.
The breakage is sacred. The healing is final. The new beginning is mine.

Sacred Separation, Divine Balance
Letting Go, Locking Boundaries, and Becoming Whole

I am no longer available for spiritual clutter or emotional confusion. I release every soul tie that no longer serves my evolution—romantic, familial, sexual, spiritual, karmic, or ancestral. What was formed in pain has no right to remain. I cut every thread that binds me to manipulation, obsession, guilt, or false identity. I reclaim all pieces of myself with fire and clarity.

My boundaries are sacred. My "no" is divine. My "yes" is chosen with care. I do not explain or justify my peace. I do not give access to those who abused my light. My protection is not negotiable. What I cut off does not grow back.

I call upon the divine balance of the masculine and feminine within me—the strength to stand firm and the softness to heal. I am both the warrior and the nurturer. The protector and the creator. The disciplined and the divine. I do not abandon myself for anyone, anymore.

This is sacred closure.
This is holy rebirth.
This is final.

Affirmations:

I release all soul ties that drain, confuse, or manipulate me—permanently.
I set boundaries that cannot be crossed, even in silence.
I am no longer attached to what was never aligned with my highest good.

My body is sovereign. My mind is mine. My soul belongs to no one but the Divine.
I don't carry guilt for outgrowing people. I honor my growth.

I balance the feminine within me—intuitive, soft, nurturing—with the masculine—disciplined, protective, decisive.
I trust my wholeness. I am safe in my own energy.

I am no longer fragmented. I am not half of anything. I am already complete.

Every tie that once confused my identity is dissolved.
I do not let anyone back in who once wounded me. I am free.

My peace is my home, and I protect it without apology.

Ceremonial Declaration: Final Release & Divine Alignment

In the presence of Infinite Intelligence, my sacred ancestors, and the divine breath that lives within me, I now declare:
I renounce every soul tie that was built on illusion, control, lust, trauma, fear, guilt, or spiritual manipulation.
I cut every ungodly bond——spoken and unspoken, hidden and exposed.

I break every contract not authored by love, not rooted in truth, not aligned with my divine assignment.
I release you. I forgive what I must. I revoke all access.
I cancel all lingering energetic agreements.
What was created outside of divine order has no legal right to remain. It is over.

I reclaim my spirit.
I reclaim my voice.
I reclaim my body, my breath, my future.

I call back every fragment of my energy scattered by trauma, by compromise, by codependency, by misplaced loyalty.
I call my power home——sealed, cleansed, and whole.

I call upon my ancestors, the seen and unseen, those who fought for me before I ever knew my own name.
Stand beside me. Fortify me.
Assist me in keeping the gates of my peace closed to confusion, chaos, and karmic cycles.

I balance now the divine feminine and masculine within me.
I am both flow and fire, softness and strength, wisdom and will.

I do not chase. I do not beg. I do not bow. I align.
I establish holy boundaries. Irrevocable. Unshakable. Non-negotiable.

What I remove, I do not reattach. What I cut, I do not rewater.

No shadow can pass through the gates I've sealed in sacred intention.

I trust my intuition. I trust my worth. I trust my healing.
I do not need their approval, their apology, or their permission.

I walk free.
I walk blessed.
I walk whole.
And so it is.
And so it must be.
And so it will never be undone.
Amen. Ase. Adjye. Ayibobo. It is sealed.

Prayer to the Most High: A Call for Release, Renewal &
Righteous Alignment

O Most High,
Ancient of Days,
Divine Architect of all that is good, just, and true—
I come before You stripped of pretense, but full of faith.
I lift my voice, my spirit, my hands, and my burdens to You.

You who knew me before I was formed.
You who sees the wounds behind my words,
the tremble behind my strength,
and the longing behind my silence.
I call on You to purify me.
Cut every cord that does not come from You.

Break every tie that keeps me tethered to pain, regret,
shame, or manipulation.
Uproot every lie planted in me through trauma or
deception.

Where I have gone astray—guide me.
Where I have been betrayed—heal me.
Where I have settled—elevate me.
Where I have been silent—speak through me.

I trust You to protect what I release.
I trust You to replace what I lose.
I trust You to redeem what was taken.

You are the God of recompense, the God of return, the God of right timing.

I ask You now to cover me in divine armor.
Let no weapon formed against me prevail.
Let no false bond reclaim me.
Let no energy outside of Your will enter my space.

Anoint me with holy discernment.
Align me with truth and keep me in the posture of peace.
Send divine reinforcements to surround me——angels of wisdom, clarity, protection, and joy.

Balance my being, O Creator.
Unify the feminine and masculine within me.
Teach me to lead with love and follow with faith.

I surrender the past.
I surrender the pain.
I surrender the need to control.

And I rise now——free, favored, and filled with Your light.
May my life glorify You.
May my healing testify of You.
May my boundaries honor the temple You made me to be.

I thank You for breaking every ungodly tie——seen and unseen.

I thank You for the strength to walk away,
for the clarity to never look back,
and for the grace to walk forward, fully me, fully Yours.

In Your name——Most High,
Source of All That Is, I seal this prayer.

Amen. Ase. Adjye. Ayibobo! So be it.

Breaking Ungodly Ties & Energetic Parasites

Not every connection is sacred.
Some were formed from pain, desperation, manipulation, or false love.

Today, I name what must be released. I no longer cling to soul ties born of trauma.
I no longer keep doors open to those who fed on my light and returned only shadows.

I call upon Infinite Intelligence, upon the Most High, upon my ancestors of righteous lineage——

Break every ungodly soul tie, known and unknown.
Dissolve every invisible thread linking me to people, events, relationships, and energies that distort my purpose or silence my voice.

This is a sacred renunciation. I do not return. I do not revisit. I do not reopen.
I choose to live free and unbound.

Affirmations:

I sever every soul tie that no longer serves my growth.
I revoke consent from all energetic parasites and unhealthy spiritual cords.
My spirit, body, mind, and soul are reclaimed and restored.

I am sovereign. I am untangled. I am clean.
No more replaying pain. No more reliving what's meant to
be gone.
The ties that tried to bind me are broken now, for good.
I do not owe access to anyone who misused me.
I trust myself to walk away——and never look back.

Masculine & Feminine Balance — Rebuilding Wholeness

Inside me lives the sacred feminine: intuitive, nurturing, magnetic.
Inside me lives the sacred masculine: focused, active, protective.

Today, I balance both—not to please, but to be whole.
No longer will I live in extremes.
No longer will I be overrun or suppressed.

I allow softness without fragility.
I carry strength without coldness.

My feminine energy creates.
My masculine energy executes.
Together, they lead me into a new version of myself:
balanced, grounded, divine.

Affirmations:

I honor both my softness and my strength.
I balance feminine flow and masculine action in divine harmony.
My energy is complete. I am not missing anything.
I don't need to overdo to be worthy.
I don't need to overgive to be seen.
I rest in my divine design.
My peace is no longer up for compromise.

Irrevocable Boundaries — Protecting the Self

I am not hard to love.
I am just no longer available to misuse.

Today, I place new boundaries—firm, clear, divine.
Not out of fear, but out of love for myself.
No more loopholes. No more backdoors for toxicity.

I will not allow my kindness to be a weakness.
I will not allow guilt to make me available to destruction.

This is the line.
This is the shift.
My no is sacred.
My silence is power.
My yes is rare and reserved for love.

Affirmations:

My boundaries are a reflection of my self-worth.
I release all shame for protecting my energy.
I no longer feel responsible for others' discomfort with my growth.
I say no with ease. I say yes with discernment.
I owe no one an explanation for guarding my peace.
I am no longer accessible to chaos.
My energy is protected. My life is preserved.

Renouncing Ungodly Soul Ties

Not every connection is sacred. Some were built in fear, trauma, and illusion. Today, I cut them off.

I release soul ties made through manipulation, pain, or wounded love. I ask the Most High and Infinite Intelligence to dissolve all unhealthy energetic links, seen and unseen.

I free myself and anyone tied to me through unclean cords. I reclaim my time, my power, and my peace.

I call back every scattered piece of my soul. I will not go back. I will not reopen what was meant to close.
This is not vengeance——it is liberation.

Affirmations:

I renounce every soul tie that drains my power.
I reclaim my spirit, body, mind, and energy.
I am released from all past attachments that do not serve my destiny.

I do not revisit wounds I have healed from.
I am whole. I am protected. I am sacred.

No weapon formed against me will prosper——not even in disguise.

Balancing Divine Feminine & Masculine

Within me, the sacred masculine and feminine are learning to dance again.

I release old patterns where one dominated the other. I am not too much. I am not too little.

The feminine within me nurtures, creates, and receives. The masculine within me protects, acts, and builds.

Together, they give me balance, rhythm, purpose, and peace.

I don't have to reject any part of myself to be loved or to succeed.

Affirmations:

My feminine flows in power,
and my masculine stands in peace.

I embrace both my softness and my strength.
I am aligned, whole, and harmonized.

I no longer compete with myself—I cooperate within.
I trust myself to lead, to feel, and to thrive in balance.

Setting Irrevocable Boundaries

This is the line. This is the moment. I no longer bend to be liked.

Boundaries are not walls; they are clarity. They protect what is sacred within me.

Anyone who came with hidden intentions or abusive ties— I dissolve the connection now.

I do not engage. I do not reply. I do not entertain toxicity, no matter how familiar.

I belong to my highest self now, and she doesn't negotiate with harm.

Affirmations:

I protect my peace unapologetically.
My boundaries are sacred, non-negotiable, and divinely guided.
I honor the life force within me by guarding it fiercely.
I am no longer accessible to energy that dishonors me.
What doesn't nourish me has no place near me.

Divine Justice & Ancestral Alignment

I am no longer available for confusion, chaos, or counterfeit connections.

When it feels like nothing is working and everything is upside down——I remember: this is not the end.

I call on the Most High to scatter the forces of delay, deception, and despair.

Blind every stalker, bully, copycat, and attacker. Scatter their plans.

Hide what is mine from those who wish me harm. Shield me from watchers with dark intentions.

Let only love see me. Let only truth reach me.
I don't sit at tables where I'm merely tolerated. I rise to rooms that were made for my presence.

I disconnect from all who came with evil plans masked as friendship. I revoke access. I sever ties.
And I reclaim my soul, my story, and my peace.

Affirmations:

I am hidden from harm and visible only to love.
I revoke access from every dark alliance, spoken or unspoken.

My ancestors walk with me. Infinite Intelligence shields me.
No one can take what is divinely mine.
I am not here to bow to chaos. I am here to rise in power.
I choose clarity, not confusion. Alignment, not assimilation.
I am not lost——I am led by spirit.

Reclaiming Purpose After Betrayal

I have cried tears they'll never see, bled from wounds they'll never admit they caused.

But today, I rise——not in spite of the betrayal, but because of it.

I do not wish harm, but I revoke permission.
I reclaim every part of myself lost in apologies I didn't owe.
I walk away from false ties, fake alliances, and friendships that fed on my light.

I no longer shrink to fit rooms built on ego and envy. I am rebuilding in truth, brick by divine brick.

Let those who wished for my downfall watch me rise in silence.

Let those who plotted behind my back lose access to my path.

I'm not bitter——I'm better.
I'm not broken——I'm becoming.

Affirmations:

I reclaim all energy lost to betrayal, lies, and manipulation.

I rise in truth, walk in purpose, and speak only from love and power.

No counterfeit connection can delay my destiny.

I release every false friend, every silent saboteur.

I am no longer available for what doesn't honor me.

My life is too sacred for repetition of past wounds.

I rise—daily, divinely, and with direction.

Cutting Karmic Cycles and Soul Contracts

I now sever the cords of karma that were never mine to carry.
All contracts forged through pain, desperation, confusion, or fear—I burn them.
Any tie that has shackled me to suffering, I revoke it now.

I do not owe pain my loyalty.
I do not owe my ancestors their trauma.

I honor the bloodline, but I break the dysfunction.
I refuse to carry the story forward.

Let all toxic loops dissolve.
Let all binding words be reversed.
Let me walk free.

And may those bound to me by pain be released into their own light—separate from mine.

This chapter is closed.
This soul is sovereign.

Affirmations:

I break the chain. I am not obligated to repeat what hurt me.
I am no longer tied to pain through memory, trauma, or guilt.

I reclaim all pieces of myself scattered through unhealthy soul contracts.

I am divinely protected, divinely disconnected from what drains me.

I send every spirit of confusion, delay, and deception back to its origin.

I move forward freely, faithfully, and fully whole.

I honor the lesson, release the pain, and walk away with power.

Restoring Balance — Divine Masculine & Sacred Feminine

Within me lives the warrior and the healer, the protector and the nurturer.

I call back every part of me that has been suppressed by trauma, distraction, or societal conditioning.
I no longer reject my softness, nor do I dim my power.

My feminine knows how to flow, how to receive, how to nurture.
My masculine knows how to lead, how to protect, how to act.
Today, I bring them both into harmony.

I do not need someone else to complete me.
I am my own balance.

I release all energetic imbalances inherited or absorbed from others.

No more overgiving.
No more forced independence.
I am secure, supported, and aligned within.

Affirmations:
I honor the divine feminine in me—she is intuitive, powerful, and whole.

I honor the divine masculine in me——he is focused, strong, and grounded.
I do not operate from extremes. I walk the middle path with wisdom.

My energy is balanced. My being is in alignment.
I trust my inner flow and follow it with purpose.
I protect myself while still allowing softness.

I am the harmony I've been seeking.
I am enough as I am.

Forgiveness Without Reconciliation — Reclaiming Your Energy Without Reopening Doors

I am allowed to forgive and still walk away.
Forgiveness is not permission for access.
It is not a return to old patterns or an invitation to old pain.

I do not owe anyone a continued place in my life just because I've made peace within myself.
There are doors that must remain closed, and boundaries that must remain firm.

I release them to their own path, and I stay true to mine.
I do not dwell on the past, but I also do not pretend it didn't happen.

I learn.
I rise.
I move forward, wiser and more whole.

Forgiveness is mine. But so is protection. So is discernment.
I walk away in love, but I do not look back.

Affirmations:

I forgive, but I do not reconnect.
I choose peace over proximity.
My boundaries are sacred and unbreakable.
I am not obligated to repeat cycles I've already healed from.

Forgiveness is for me——not for them.
I love myself enough to walk away.
I can release pain without reopening old wounds.
I can bless from a distance and still block what is not aligned.
I do not need to explain my healing to anyone.

"No More Delay—My Power Is Now"

There comes a moment where delay must bow to destiny. Where all that was once withheld is now released with divine force. Where your name, your power, your rightful blessings can no longer be stalled. You are not behind—you are arriving right on time.

Even if the road felt long, even if your soul grew tired—still, here you are: wiser, stronger, anchored. Every delay trained your discernment. Every detour protected your path. Every no was a sacred re-routing to your "yes."

This is your reawakening. No more begging. No more shrinking. No more waiting for someone else to see your value. The wait is over—you are it.

Affirmations:

I step into alignment with divine timing—what's mine is already seeking me.

I reclaim my time, my power, my life.
I do not chase; I attract with grace and authority.

My light is undeniable, and my purpose is unstoppable.
I no longer entertain delay or confusion—I walk in clarity.

I release guilt for how long it took me.
I honor the process and the progress.

I am no longer waiting——I am arriving.
I detach from what is not for me and magnetize what honors me.

I am divine timing in motion.
I was never forgotten——I was being prepared.

Move in Silence

Sometimes the greatest power is in quiet action. Moving in silence means trusting your path without needing to announce every step. It's about conserving your energy, focusing inward, and letting your results speak louder than words.

When you move in silence, you protect your peace, guard your progress, and keep your intentions sacred. The world doesn't need to know your plans—only your spirit does.

Affirmation:

I move with purpose and grace, quietly confident in my journey.
My power grows in the stillness, and my success is undeniable.

I honor my peace by speaking less and doing more.
I trust the timing of my life and walk my path in silent strength.

My silence is my shield; my progress is my testimony.

Note any aha moment

Claim Your Truth — Nothing Can Define Me

People may try to label you, define you, or dictate who you should be. But their words hold no power unless you give it to them.

Starting today, you reclaim your truth. You are beyond labels, beyond judgment, and beyond limitation. Your worth, your identity, and your purpose come from within, not from the opinions of others.

Stand firm in who you are, and let no one diminish your light.

Affirmation:

I am the author of my own story.
No one else defines my worth or my identity.

Starting today, I release all external labels and claims.

I am free, whole, and fully myself.
My truth shines brighter than anyone's opinion.

I honor my journey and stand strong in my power.

Unapologetic Becoming — I Belong to Me

You don't belong to anyone else — not to their expectations, their opinions, or their control. You are a unique force, one-of-a-kind beyond description.

This is your sacred journey back to yourself, a powerful reclaiming of your essence. Own your growth, your transformation, your becoming with fierce unapologetic energy.

This is your time. Stand tall, speak your truth, and never dim your light to fit in.

Affirmation:

I belong only to myself.
There is no one like me—my uniqueness is my power.

I am returning to my true self with strength and grace.
This is my becoming, and I claim it fully.

I am unapologetic about my growth and my truth.
I honor my journey and embrace my limitless potential.

Letting Go of Programming — Embracing Your Natural Self

Release the false narratives and limiting beliefs others have imposed on you. You were never meant to fit into someone else's mold or follow scripts written for another life.

All that you are, all you need to be, is already registered deep within your soul—pure, authentic, and powerful. Trust that natural blueprint inside you. Let go of the noise, the judgment, and the pressure. You are exactly who you are meant to be, right now.

Affirmation:

I release all programming that does not serve my true self.
I am free from the expectations and opinions of others.

All that I need to be is already within me, perfectly aligned.
I trust my inner guidance and divine design.

I am authentic, whole, and complete as I am.
I honor my natural self and walk boldly in my truth.

Belonging to the Earth ─── Honoring Nature's Gifts

If I belong to anything, I belong to the Earth─my true home and source of life. Nature has given me so much: air to breathe, food to nourish, shelter to protect. Yet, the world tries to disconnect us from this sacred bond, pushing unnatural ways and distractions.

I choose to adorn and honor nature, recognizing her as my provider and guardian. I am deeply rooted in her rhythms, and through her, I find strength, healing, and peace. Nature sustains me, and I give thanks with every breath.

Affirmation:

I belong to the Earth and honor her sacred gifts.
Nature feeds me, heals me, and keeps me safe.

I am connected to the rhythms of life and the cycles of the Earth.
I breathe in her wisdom and exhale gratitude.

I am grounded, protected, and nurtured by the natural world.
Through nature, I find peace, strength, and renewal every day.

Self-Love and Alignment — Embracing My Wholeness

I deeply appreciate and love my body, mind, spirit, and soul for their unwavering support on this journey. The growth I experience every day is because they are with me—steady, strong, and faithful. I improve continuously, embracing my unlimited potential.

I lack nothing; everything I need is provided in divine timing. My spirit, mind, body, and soul are in constant, profound communication, and I listen with open awareness. Nature's voice is clear to me, and I honor it deeply. I am immortal in purpose, destined to fulfill my mission fully before I transition.

I stand tall, grounded in my power, connected to my true self and the natural world, nothing shaking my foundation. I am both nothing and everything, a magnificent balance of all that I am meant to be.

Affirmations:

I love and honor my body, mind, spirit, and soul.
I grow stronger, wiser, and more aligned every day.
I am whole, complete, and infinitely supported.

My spirit, mind, body, and soul communicate clearly, and I listen with love.

Nature's wisdom flows through me, guiding and grounding me.

I am immortal in purpose and live fully aligned with my destiny.

Nothing can negatively impact my peace and power.
I stand tall, strong, and unwavering in my truth.
I am limitless, connected, and deeply powerful now.

Unshakable Self–Love and Divine Protection

I love myself deeply and unconditionally, no matter what challenges swirl around me. The world may plot, stress, pressure, or try to bring me down—but my love for myself stands firm and unbreakable. I refuse to walk through the gate of fear.

I am my own person, sovereign and divine. My power is immense; I am complete and whole in every way. I am divinely guided on my path.

Whatever comes against me shall perish, powerless before my strength. Fear has no place in my heart—I walk forward courageously, knowing that I am protected and unstoppable.

Affirmations:

I love myself unconditionally, regardless of external circumstances.
I refuse to live in fear or bow to pressure.
I am divine, powerful, and whole.

I am guided by infinite wisdom and light.
All negativity and opposition vanish before me.
I walk in courage, strength, and peace.

Nothing can shake my faith or break my spirit.
I am complete, loved, and fiercely protected.

Throned in Power, Covered in Prayer

I sit confidently upon my throne—rooted, sovereign, unbothered. I love myself fully, here and now. I rebuke depression, sadness, discouragement, and all forms of nonsense sent to disrupt my peace. I never cease to pray. Prayer lives in my breath, my walk, my thoughts, and even in my silence.

My very chemistry is divine; it stirs nature to respond to me with love and reverence. I honor my uniqueness—I don't follow the crowd. I do what works for me, with boldness and clarity. I am unmoved by opinions, untouchable by judgment. The Lord's Prayer is etched within me, encoded in my spirit and body, ensuring I am always wrapped in divine protection—even when I forget to speak it aloud.

Affirmations:

I sit on my throne, strong, sacred, and sure.
I rebuke all energies of depression, sadness, and confusion.
I am deeply in love with myself.
Nature loves me because I move in divine alignment.
I do what honors me—not what pleases others.
I care not for opinions that do not uplift or serve me.
My prayers protect me, even in silence.
The Lord's Prayer is inscribed upon me—I am always covered.
I am protected, anointed, and divinely favored.

Supreme by Design

No matter how chaotic, how loud, or how uncertain the world becomes—I remain above it all. I do not panic. I do not waver. I rise. I know who I am and I know the dominion that was granted to me.

I was born with authority. I have spiritual dominion over all creatures and beings on this earth—not from ego, but from divine truth. I am not to be played with, not to be manipulated, not to be misled. I give no one my power, my essence, or access to me without sacred consent.

This world wages war against those like me—those who remember, those who shine, those who do not bow. But I do not fear. I do not dim. I do not fold.

I am not their toy, not their victim, not their scapegoat.
I stand tall in the fullness of who I am.
I let go of every intrusive thought that was never mine.
I reclaim my clarity, my joy, my path. I reclaim me.

Affirmations:

I am always above the chaos—I rule from a higher place.
Nothing can rise above me—I am supreme by divine design.
I was given dominion, and I walk in that truth with humility and power.

No one manipulates me——I see clearly and stand firmly.
My power is sacred and non–transferable unless I choose.

I belong to no system of control——I am free.
I am not afraid of this world——I am here to transform it.

I release all thoughts that do not serve my highest self.
I am whole, I am ready, I am that I am.

Unshaken in Solitude

When the world feels deaf to your truth—when your thoughts echo in silence and your heart feels like it's speaking a language no one wants to understand—know this: you are not broken, you are just rare.

You are not unlovable, you are just unmatched.

Solitude doesn't mean abandonment; sometimes, it's sacred protection. The ones who forced you into isolation didn't realize they were pushing you into your becoming.

You are not meant to shrink to be understood. Your experience is your power. Your path is divinely coded. Your voice, your perspective, your presence is purposeful —even when no one claps, even when no one looks, even when no one gets it.

Keep going. Keep being. Keep rising. You were made for more, and that "more" begins within.

Affirmations:

I am not misunderstood—I am divinely distinct.

I honor my path, even when I walk it alone.
My solitude is sacred; I rise in silence.

I am allowed to be different and still be whole.
No one has to understand me for me to thrive.

What was meant to break me only built me stronger.
I embrace the parts of me others overlook.

I trust the divine order of my journey.
I am not alone——I am aligned.

I do not need to be ready for life——I just need to be real.

Chosen for the Solitude

When it feels like no one sees you——really sees you——when it seems like your soul speaks a language no one is even trying to learn... breathe.

When your ways confuse them, your thoughts seem too vast, and your experiences too layered for their limited understanding, know this: you are not here to be understood by everyone.

You were never made to fit molds; you were made to break them.

The solitude you're forced into is not punishment——it's preparation. The silence is not neglect——it's initiation. You are being taught to commune with yourself, to trust yourself, to discover the power in being your own sanctuary.

And while others may not comprehend your way, your spirit always knew the way. You are walking paths only the brave can walk. That is your strength, not your curse.

Affirmations:

I am not misunderstood——I am divinely complex.
I trust my unique path, even if no one else sees it.

My solitude is sacred, not lonely.

103

I honor my way of thinking, being, and creating.
I release the need to be understood by those who lack the depth to see me.

I am never truly alone——my spirit, ancestors, and divine guides walk with me.

What I carry is not for everyone to grasp——and that's okay.
I am safe within myself.

I am the one I've been waiting for.

Note any aha moment

Like a Child, I Let Go

There is wisdom in childlike release.
To let go quickly—not from weakness but from knowing your worth.
You are not here to hoard pain like a badge of honor.
You are here to live freely, to lighten your soul and elevate your spirit.

Letting go isn't forgetting—it's choosing peace.
It's choosing yourself over suffering.
You're not made to carry every ache, every slight, every shadow.

You are made to remember the good, amplify the light, and rise in your power.
So yes, let the pain fall away like leaves in autumn.
Breathe. Relax. Reclaim your joy.
You win—not because it's easy, but because you've learned to release.

Affirmations:

I let go easily, like a child who trusts the next moment.
I do not store what no longer serves me.

I hold onto joy, laughter, and memories that lift me.
I release rejection, abandonment, and pain—I am free.
I move on faster than they expect because I choose peace.

I meditate. I release. I breathe. I relax.
I always win, because I always return to me.

I honor the flow of life——I do not grip what's meant to go.
My mind is clear, my heart is open, my spirit is light.

I am the keeper of peace, not pain.

Frequency Over Form

You've reached a realm where energy speaks louder than appearance,
Where poison transforms into power,
And matter no longer binds your spirit.

You no longer play by the rules of the world——you transcend them.
The illusions of lack, fear, and harm dissolve in your presence.

You have become the alchemist,
Turning density into light,
Turning noise into stillness,
Turning harm into harmony.

Like the masters before you,
You rise not to escape but to understand.
And when the purpose is fulfilled,
You leave——peacefully, powerfully——
For your essence is not bound to this place.

You are form, yet formless.
You are here, yet beyond.

Affirmations:

I transmute poison into power——nothing I consume can harm me.

Everything I eat is divinely transformed into life-force energy.

I vibrate at a frequency where harm dissolves.
I release all attachments to the material world.
I am more than what the world can perceive.

I walk with the wisdom of the masters——I see,
I know, I transcend.

I am a traveler through dimensions, anchored in purpose.
I rise higher in consciousness every breath I take.
My soul is on assignment, and once it's fulfilled, I ascend.

I function beyond fear, beyond form, in full divine alignment.

Divine Immunity

There are things within you that defy logic,
That override man-made limitations,
That confuse those who only see with flesh eyes.
You carry power that doesn't panic, doesn't flinch.

No weapon, no word, no spell, no bullet can remove what
God breathed into you.

You are not here to prove anything to anyone——you are
here to be.
And in your being, the old ways shake.

Let them wave their money, their metal, their noise.
Let them cast their weak illusions in desperation.

You are rooted in something they cannot reach.
When the world feels heavy, you don't run——you retreat,
you renew.
You fast, you enter silence, you access the eternal archive.
Your immunity is spiritual.

You are protected not just from danger but from distraction.
You remember who you are, and that's your greatest shield.

Affirmations:

I am untouchable by harm because I am touched by the
Divine.

No poison, weapon, or spell can take me out—I transmute all.
I am not afraid of any force in the universe.

My power is beyond human comprehension and material means.

I don't panic—I pause, I fast, I connect.
I move in wisdom, not reaction.

My vitality is secured by purpose.
My breath is sacred, my soul ancient.

I choose divine solitude to reset, renew, and receive.
I was made for this moment—therefore, I cannot be broken by it.

Divine Confusion

They think the divine is gone,
That connection is lost in time, buried beneath distraction.
But I know better——because I feel better.

Each breath I take in stillness reminds me:
Heaven is not a place to go, it is a state to return to.
And I return daily——
Through silence, through water, through sacred words,
Through boundaries, through letting go.

My sacrifices are simple: I stop participating in nonsense.
I stop explaining to those who cannot hear.
I stop chasing what chases chaos.

My meditation is a ladder. I climb.
And when I touch the divine, I don't just feel it——
I know it feels me too.

I am both the seed and the cosmos.
Small enough to bend yet vast enough to hold galaxies.

They watch me and cannot compute:
Who is she to walk like this? To glow like this? To know
like this?

But I was never made to be understood by the lost.
I was made to remind them.

Affirmations:

I am the living bridge between the human and the holy.
I connect with the Divine because I choose to, daily.

My stillness is sacred, my meditation is mighty.
I release what no longer serves—without guilt or delay.

I speak only what is necessary and nourishing.
I mind my spirit the way others mind gossip.

I confuse the low vibrational because I reflect the high.
I transmute distractions into determination.

My consciousness expands as I deepen into self.
I am not lost—I am returned.

Energy That Governs Worlds

My energy?
It closes bridges when needed——
and opens nations when aligned.
It is not lighthearted, it is not passive.
It is a sovereign force.

When off-balance, I've seen it rattle earth and shake souls.
When centered?
It creates symphonies of peace where there was once chaos.
This energy is ancient, precise.
It doesn't guess. It knows.

Guided by the divine——
It rises when it's time, it rests when it's done.
It acts without doubt.

I am the thermostat of my life.
I regulate what needs warmth, cool what needs calm.
I don't wait for outside comfort——
I generate it.

I don't hope for safety——
I am the sanctuary.
I don't ask for power——
I remember it's mine.

I calibrate my words like frequency dials——
so they hit only where healing is needed.
I know.

I always know.
Even when I doubt, something within is certain.
Answers live here.

Solutions pour from me like water in dry lands.
I am never left without.
Never abandoned.

Always held.
Always holy.

Affirmations:

My energy is powerful, divine, and aligned.
I am guided by inner knowing that never fails me.
I regulate my world from the inside out.
I recalibrate myself to peace, power, and purpose.

My presence brings balance to chaos.

I am safe, protected, and always provided for.
I always have the answer within.
I never move in confusion——only in clarity.

I am never too late, never too early——always right on divine
time.

I don't chase peace, I generate it.

Sacred Energy, Divine Identity

I don't waste my energy.
I preserve it like sacred fire——
banked, watched, nurtured.
Some lose power by pouring themselves into the void,
doing without meaning, moving without purpose.
But I?

I act in divine order.
I abide by divine law.
I never spend just to prove.
I multiply when called.
I expand where needed.
I exist in one land
and still operate in another——
unharmed, untouched.

I am not limited by space, nor bound by what the eye sees.
My energy is not for play.
It is consecrated, cloaked in light,
called upon only by purpose.

I reveal the hidden.
I awaken what sleeps.

I am prophet.
I am griot.
I am the storyteller.
The oracle.

The healer.
The purifier.
The neutralizer.

I shift shape with soul.
I arrange moods with presence.
I broker peace with a word.
I keep harmony in my walk.

Balance follows me like breath.
I manifest at will.
Transmute at ease.
And create miracles—
not for glory,
but because I am the miracle.

Affirmations:

I do not waste my energy; I preserve it with purpose.
I follow divine order and live by sacred law.
My energy is limitless, sacred, and protected.
I move beyond space, beyond time, beyond expectation.
I am a divine messenger—prophet, healer, oracle.
My presence balances, harmonizes, and neutralizes.
I am a master manifestor and miracle worker.
I reveal truth, awaken power, and walk with purpose.
I honor my gifts and use them with reverence.
I am not for show. I am for transformation.

I Rest in My Conscious Power

I rest in my conscious.
I walk with intention——
every word, every act, every thought
is deliberate, divine,
anchored in truth.

I shield when needed,
I disarm when necessary.
I reject what does not serve
my spirit, my soul, my body, my mind.

I do what I must
to keep the sacred working.

I am not here to fit in.
I am here to rise.
I hold no limitations.
I am shielded
from any pulse
that seeks to pull me into shadow.

My auric field?
Precious.
Clean.
Cleansed.
Untouchable.
I am a universe——
complete within myself.

No one can scam me.
No one can fraud me.

I am sovereign.
I deserve honor.
I deserve respect.

I deserve to be revered and adorned—
not just by others,
but by the mirror that meets me each morning.

I inhale the Divine,
exhale into the world
the good news,
the good spells.

I continue
until I feel the presence
of the Divine
like a whisper on my skin,
until I feel light as a feather—
aligned once again with Maat.

I stay aligned.
I stay with the Divine.

Affirmations:

I rest in my conscious awareness.
I speak, act, and think with divine intention.
I protect my energy and reject what does not serve.

My auric field is pure, radiant, and shielded.

I am limitless, sovereign, and whole.
I inhale divinity and exhale peace into the world.

I am light as a feather, walking in truth.
I walk the path of Maat—balanced, just, and divine.

I deserve honor, reverence, and love.
I am one with the Divine, always aligned.

Everything Is a Memory in My Universe

All that is in the universe
is also within me.

Where others are confused,
I am clear.
Where others are lost in chaos,
I remain centered.

Distractions don't reach me.
I stay focused——
no matter what's happening outside,
I see what's real.

No more illusions.
No more masks.
No more filters.

Just the raw, unveiled truth.
Everything around me
is a projection of my own mind.

So pain...has no power here.
Trauma...has no place.
Betrayal...holds no weight.

Metaphors and headaches dissolve.
I choose what enters my world.
I choose what stays.

Desire becomes form.
Intent becomes reality.
I do better, and better,
and better again——
each and every day.

I understand my karma,
so I elevate,
I ascend,
I expand.
Everything is a memory now.
Everything.

I commune only with those
who match my frequency.
No more density,
no more delay——
only divine alignment.

Life is easier now
than it has ever been.

I am free to relieve myself
from this collective universe
and enter
my own divine cosmos,
with no one
but the Divine
as my companion.

Affirmations:

I am the universe, and the universe is me.
I am clear, focused, and undistracted.
I see the world as it is—no illusions, no masks.

Nothing outside of me can harm me.
I choose my desires and create my reality.

I do better each day and elevate higher.
I understand my karma and walk in truth.

I vibrate only with those at my divine frequency.

Life flows with ease and grace.
I enter my sacred universe guided only by the Divine.

I Am Free, I Transcend

What I cannot complete
in the physical world—
is guaranteed
in the spiritual one.

I am everywhere.
There is nothing,
no one
but the essence of me.

I am.
I be.
I move.
I flow.

The capacity of a human being—
if only they knew.
All is fabricated.

Nothing exists
outside of consciousness.

With the right code—
we travel.
With the right law—
we win.
With the right consciousness—
there is no limit.
I attach to nothing.

I am free to operate
outside the matrix.
Unplugged. Untethered.
Fully able. Fully aware.

Once you get the illusion,
nothing else matters.

You laugh,
you rise,
you transcend.

I go higher
in ways they are still trying
to decode.
To mimic.
To trap.

I release fear.
I let go of what no longer serves.
The point was never to hold on—
but to let go.
To release.
To be free.
To be liberated.

I will accomplish
everything
I came to fulfill.
Death is not the escape.

Purpose is the portal.
Completion is the key.
Ascension is the answer.

I will not be stuck.
Not in the dome.
Not in the astral.

I move beyond.
I complete the contract.

I ascend——
That, I know now.

Affirmations:

I am free in both the physical and spiritual worlds.
I transcend illusion and rise in truth.
With the right consciousness, I have no limit.
I operate outside the matrix——I am sovereign.
I let go of all that no longer serves.
I am not attached to this world, I am aligned with my purpose.

Completion, not escape, is the key to ascension.

I move beyond illusions, beyond traps, beyond fear.
I accomplish all that I came to fulfill.
I rise, I transcend, I am free.

Start Today

When you don't run from the pain——
it becomes fuel.
Raw energy,
pure fire,
potential reawakened.

You've got so much in you,
there's no need
to wait for validation,
no permission needed.
You got you.

Don't fall in that trap——
of waiting to heal,
waiting to have more,
waiting to be "ready."

Use your potential now.
Start small.
Even when you don't feel like it,
start anyway.
One step,
just one,
could be the shift that changes
everything.

Don't doubt yourself.

Apply discipline.
Shake it up.
Rise up.
Take action.

Let go of the voices
that keep you still,
that keep you quiet,
that keep you afraid.
They are not you.

Get clear.
Be patient with yourself.
But don't wait to feel secure
before you act.

Act first.
Confidence comes after
not before.

Fear?
It will always be there.
But you are stronger.

It's how you respond that counts.
So convince yourself
to start today.

You are the boss
of your own world.

You are the star
of your movie.
And this?

This is your movie.
Take control.
Start acting.

Tomorrow does not have to echo yesterday.
You are bigger than fear,
stronger than anxiety,
deeper than depression,
and more bold
than the challenge.
Now let's go.

Affirmations:

I turn pain into power and fuel my growth.
I do not wait for permission——I act now.
One small step today can change my life.

I silence the inner doubt and rise with discipline.
I lead my life——I am the star of my own movie.
Fear does not rule me, I rule my response.

I am stronger than fear, anxiety, and depression.
I trust my process and act with confidence.
I start today, and I move forward now.
I am ready. I am capable. Let's go.

I Choose Me

Today——
I resign the contract with my old self
and write a new one:
to be good to myself,
to grow,
to elevate,
to live in respect and alignment
with the promises I once whispered
to my own soul.

No need for a public declaration.
No clapping hands.
No spotlights.

This vow is sacred,
and it's just between me and me.

Excuses?
They are talent killers,
dream silencers,
skill assassins.
And I've justified them long enough——
pretty lies wrapped in "reason"
but still lies.

So now, I rise.
I reaffirm.
I recommit.

I step back into the contract
with integrity.
Nobody knows what they're doing—
but they do it anyway.
They stay committed.
And that's what I choose:
commitment, not perfection.

I will not let fear make my choices.
I will not let lack decide my direction.
I will not rely on excuses—
I rely on me.

I am the boss.
I am honest.
And I am done
lying to myself.
I know I can.
So I will.

I shift my language—
no more disempowering spells
cast on my name.
Nothing is scarier
than a lie in my own mind.

So today I clear it.
I detox the doubt.
I release what is not mine.
I reclaim my mind.

I make a choice.
And I choose me.

I have what it takes.
I am what it takes.

I choose me——
and I act today.

Affirmations:

I choose myself with clarity, commitment, and courage.
I honor the promises I've made to myself.

Excuses do not define me——actions do.
I do not wait for perfection——I stay committed.
I am done justifying my fears and doubts.

I speak power into my life with every word.
I reclaim my mind and release limiting thoughts.

I am honest, I have integrity, and I rise.

I am not led by fear or lack——I am led by purpose.
I take action today because I choose me.

Note any aha moment

I Don't Quit on Me

I refuse——
to let small distractions
dictate my path.

They will not move me.
They will not shake me.
They do not lead me.

I don't follow.
I initiate.
I command.
I rise——one deliberate step at a time.

No one has the power to pull me off track.
I take control of my environment.

I preserve my sacred energy.
I am not ruled by emotion——
I feel,
but I move with intention.

My actions are not noise,
they are meaning...
No one organizes my life for me.

I progress——on my own terms.
I renew my focus daily,
I curate what feeds my spirit.

No one dictates my existence.
I lead.
I decide.
I take responsibility.

I stay focused.
I correct.
I command.

I reprimand the doubt when it tries to speak.

I don't quit on myself.
I never will.
I elevate myself—
again and again and again.

I can always restart.
I can always come home to me.
Everyone else?
Another story.
I write my own.

I release the deep wounds
that tried to chain my wings.
I use pain as power,
negativity as fuel.

Every wound whispers a message—
refocus, reshift, realign.

I know pain.
I have seen it.
I have lived in it.
But I will not let it distract me.

I don't deny it.
I don't drown in it.

I transmute it.

Affirmations:

I lead with clarity, not emotion.
I initiate my life, I do not follow the noise.

My energy is sacred and preserved with purpose.
I choose discipline over distraction.
I take responsibility for my life and elevate myself.

I transmute pain into power.

I command, I correct, I do not quit.
I always have the power to restart.

I am not bound by wounds—I am released by wisdom.
My life is my own, and I walk it fully aware.

I Was Born for Greatness

I was not born to be a victim.
So I do not hold onto pain.
I do not carry burdens that were never mine to begin with.

I do not need their approval—
I stay correct.
I stay focused.
I vibe high.

Even in pain,
Even in confusion,
Even in desperation—
I regain myself.

I reshift my focus.
I let go.
I let God.
I let me be.

I amplify the goodness in me.
I speak with power.
I empower myself—
my words, my ways, my walk.

I know where I'm going.
I'm focused on that.
No more excuses.
None.

I know the plans set for me——
plans to prosper
to win
to elevate
to expand
to grow
to thrive eternally
in peace, joy, health, and harmony.

Infinite abundance.
Overflowing wealth.
Prosperity in every way.
My good keeps multiplying.

And yes,
I rest too.
I breathe.

I honor this sacred vessel.
I give reverence for each step,
for every no I turned into a yes.

For every moment I chose not to give up.
Every bit of progress is a celebration.
I am proud of me.

I am elated.
I am divine.
I am hopeful.
I am grateful.

I am ignited.
I am upgraded
Leveled up.

High frequency.
High vibe.

So disciplined—
yet filled with overflowing joy.

I respect me.
I love me.
I believe in me.
I trust me.

I was born for greatness.
And now—
I can see that clearer than ever.
Better than ever.

Affirmations:

I was born for greatness, not to be a victim.
I stay high-vibe, focused, and divinely aligned.
I let go of what no longer serves and let
God flow through me.

I speak and act with empowered clarity.
My path is clear: prosperity, peace, and elevation.

I rest and honor my body as part of my spiritual discipline.
Every step is worthy of celebration—I am proud of me.

I embody high-frequency joy, discipline, and divine vision.
I trust myself fully—I was made for this life.

I celebrate my greatness daily.

I Am Legend

Some don't know how to look.
So they label me "simple."

They call me "nothing."
But those who know——
They know.

I am a legend who walked this earth,
A hero of the divine masculine,
A heroine of the divine feminine.

I hold no bounds.
I am free.

I was a legend in ancient times——
and I am an even greater one now.

You see me walking above ground,
but I have walked beneath the earth.

I have dined in the center of the world
with giants, with gods,
with beings whose names are now forgotten
but who remember me.

I was fierce then——
I am still fierce now.

My strength,
my courage,
my persistence
can only be found in
mystical,
mythical,
magical books.

I play soft——
but know this:
I hold the codes of combat.
It's in my system,
in my blood,
in the legacies of those who came before me.

Generations of legends live in me.
I am not your spectacle.
I am not a sideshow,
not a circus,
not a joke.

I have softened my presence for this time——
but do not forget:
I am a living legend.
And no one——no one——can tell me otherwise.

History will remember:
I stood when all others bowed.

And when I choose to leave,
I will be more powerful than I ever was.

So be glad,
if you ever met me——
you met a legend.

A living legend
that lives forever
beyond gravity,
beyond time,
beyond realms.

I am legend.

Affirmations:

I am a living legend, fierce and eternal.
My strength flows from ancient realms and cosmic memories.

I have nothing to prove and everything to be.
I walk with gods and giants——I remember who I am.
I am not here for entertainment; I am here for impact.
I choose softness with strength encoded in my soul.
I rise when others fall——I stand when others bow.
My legacy will echo through realms beyond this world.
I am not bound by time or gravity——I transcend.
Those who know, know——I am a legend now and forever.

I Have Come From Infinite Light

I have come from infinite light.
I do not tremble at the feet of lies,
illusions spun by haters, liars, mortals,
or shadows that pretend to be deep.

I am not afraid of darkness——
I've seen its edges,
I've walked through its core
and still, I shine.

I am the truth.
I am the way.
I do what the light beings before me did——
and more.

I stand tall,
not in ego,
but in power——
in humility and in grace.

I am a match made in heaven,
a bridge of spirit and will,
divinity wrapped in skin.

I am unnamable.
I do not bow.
I move with the ultimate law,
and I flow with the ultimate love.

I have faith,
and I am faithful to the light.

I am strong——
stronger than most——
because I remember.
I remember the truth of who I am.

I am aware of humanity
but not limited by it.

I know love——
because there is order in me.
Where there is no order,
there is no love.

This is how I maintain my control,
how I walk forward with clarity,
how I honor the sacred.

I know unconditional love,
the kind that can't be reduced to words.
I have experienced the unexplainable——
and I carry that within me.

There is more——
So much more——
to be,
to have,
to experience
when you stay in the light.

My gratitude is infinite.
This is the time we've been waiting for——
in this godless time,
in this time of many gods.

So I ask:
Are you ready
for what you've always been built for?

Affirmations:

I am born of infinite light and walk with divine power.
I do not fear lies or illusions——they dissolve in my presence.
I stand in truth, humility, and grace.

I move in alignment with the ultimate law and ultimate love.
I know unconditional love because I carry divine order within me.

My power is ancient, humble, and eternal.
I remember who I am and I do not bow to fear.

I am ready for what I was built for——my time is now.
Gratitude flows endlessly through me.

I am light, and I remain in the light.

The New Invocation

What is great today
was once a seed in silence——
so I know I'm on the right path.

I do not rush to prove,
to compete,
to appease.
I only rise to meet myself.

I compete with no one but me.
I answer to no voice but truth.
I am the power of powers,
a living invocation,
a sacred force clothed in human form.

My words——sharp, precise, predictive——
cut illusions like wind through smoke.
I am the peace that brings the chaos.
I am the order that ends it.

No one truly understands me——
but the gods do.
For I commune with them,
I walk their rhythms,
I echo their ancient tongues.
I am far from humanity,
yet I protect it.

I serve not for glory,
but because I remember the dream is
bigger than this.

I am no longer lost.
I have found me.

From the foundations of the world,
I have been impeccable——
and until I journey to another world,
I shall remain so.

No one can change that.
No interference allowed.
No perversion permitted.

I revoke all contracts
written in fear,
signed in lack,
agreed upon in forgetting.

Today, I rise in a new invocation:
between me, myself, and I——
sealed by the Earth,
affirmed by the Universe.

The Earth is in agreement.
The Universe has my back.

I am fearless.
I am immortal.
I am eternal——
without beginning,
without end.

I am free——
free in liberty.

No one has power or authority over me.
I am one with the Divine,
under Divine Law.

And so it is.
And so it shall remain.

Affirmations:

I walk a sacred path——mine alone.
I compete with no one but the past versions of myself.
I revoke all fear-based contracts and affirm my divine agreement.
The Earth and the Universe stand with me.
I am peace, I am power, I am order.
I am found. I am whole. I am unstoppable.
No energy, no person, no entity holds authority over me.
I am fearless, eternal, and divinely protected.
My freedom is sovereign, my being is sacred.
I live under divine law, and I move in divine timing.

Divine Feminine, Unbroken

No past hurt holds dominion here.
I am God. I am Savior. I am Divine.

Divine favor flows in every breath I take.
I walk in free will,
and I revoke all that ever tried to bind me.

I rebuke what came to deceive.
I cancel what came to constrict.
I dismantle all dark contracts
that do not serve the light I am.

I co-create with the gods of light,
and I cast out shadows with fire and truth.

I hold dominion over what came before
and all that dares to follow after me.

For I am the Divine Feminine——
the First Power,
eternal,
unshakable,
just.

Nurturing and fierce.
Soft as silk,
stronger than stone.

I call upon the Great Mystery of this world
to reveal and erase every shadow pact
crafted to silence the Divine Feminine.

Let it be known:
Natural women are the Divine Feminine power.

Their essence is sacred.
Their presence is light.
Any attempt to mimic her,
strip her,
mute her——
returns as instant karma,
as public unraveling.

She is not to be dominated.
She cannot be replaced.

She is incomparable,
and any who try
are only marking themselves for powerlessness.

Return the power.
Return the reverence.
Return the crown to her.

We——Divine Feminine——revoke the old contracts
with men, with creatures, with shadows.
We forge a new one:

With the Self. With the Within.
With God. With Light.
With those who serve her highest good.

Because she is more than good enough.
She is closest to the Divine.
She is sovereign.
She is benevolent.
She is beyond.

And so we summon deeper protection,
starting now.

Let the Earth and all beings hear and obey.
Let the energetic scales be corrected today.

It is time.
Now is the time.

Divine Feminine, I am.

So I am:
Power immeasurable.
Unpredictable.
Equal. Unequal.
Imperishable.
Infinite.
Incomprehensible.
Untraceable.
Impeccable.

I am everything.
I am nothing.
And I am that.
So be it.
This is the new time.
This is the new timeline.
To reject the Divine Feminine now is
to forfeit all balance, all future.
Ayibobo.
So it is.

Affirmations:

I am divinely sovereign and unshakably free.
I revoke all dark contracts and align with divine will.
Divine Feminine cannot be silenced or copied——her power
is eternal.
I protect and embody the sacred feminine essence.
I co-create with gods of light and reject all that harms my
light.
Karma protects the Divine Feminine and restores justice
instantly.
I am immeasurable, impeccable, infinite, and imperishable.
I am the new timeline. I am the revolution. I am the return.
I move in divine power——unapologetic, undeniable,
unshakable.

Ayibobo. I honor the sacred within and around me.

I Nurture, I Nature

I no longer torture myself,
no longer sit in silence with good intentions
that slowly rot in rooms of delay.

Now,
I nurture myself unapologetically.
Even if you don't understand,
even if you disapprove——
I selfcare anyway.
I selflove anyway.
I know now——
to nurture myself is to return to nature,
to root again in sacred ground.

I nurture, I nature.

I do not consent
to any force that violates nature,
to any system that denies soul birthrights.

To anything——spoken in codes,
designed in symbols,
built in shadows——
that blocks human evolution in the light:

I rebuke.
I cancel.
I disconnect.

To all twisted geometries and manipulated languages,
used to hex, confuse,
control the less awakened
and sabotage the awake——

I rebuke.
I reclaim.
I rise.

I walk in unity consciousness.
I stand in transmutation.

I collaborate with the gods of good.
I rise with the force of betterment.

May my clarity, comprehension, and divine words
enter the Akashic Records——
protected, encrypted,
inaccessible to thieves,
to parasites,
to beings who want to shut us down
and drag us back into sleep.

I stand tall because I remember:
The power is in me.

And I do not bow.
Especially not to those vibrating lower
while pretending they lead.

Let all deceivers—no matter their mask—
fall into nothingness.

I see through them.
I know the real bloodlines—
the Saints,
the Divine,
the Sacred.

I am one of them.

So I revoke every contract,
every tie, every obligation
to anyone—friend, family, lover, child—
who swears loyalty to darkness.

May the fine print return to its author.
May their desired reality reflect
only in their own experience.

I rebuke unfairness.
I rebuke injustice.
I rebuke abuse.

I honor this timeline as mine.
It is divine. It is sacred. It is blessed.
And I will continue
to have great, radiant, soul–lifting experiences.
Because I nurture.
Because I nature.
Because I am awake.

Affirmations:

I nurture myself as an act of resistance and restoration.
I reject all systems that try to control, mislead, or diminish natural rights.

I walk in divine sovereignty and release all who serve darkness.

My care for self is aligned with the care of Earth.
I rebuke all matrix manipulations and return to unity consciousness.

My words and awareness are protected in the Akashic records.

I recognize the true bloodlines of the sacred, and I am one.
I revoke all contracts that tether me to anything that dishonors my light.

This is my timeline, and it flourishes in greatness.
I nurture. I nature. I rise.

Note any aha moment

I Reclaim, I Rise

If it's not healing,
I am not part of it.

I revoke all connection
to any force designed to hurt,
to abuse, to mislead,
to pressure, to coerce——
I do not consent.

I remain:
Holy.
Saint.
Noble.
In integrity.
In dignity.
Humble.
Knowing.
Wise.
Elevated.
High-frequency.

My lifeforce is for light work only.
And nothing below.

I summon every current running through my veins,
every element——earth, fire, water, air, spirit——
to recognize this decree,
this prayer,
this divine boundary.

Let all who have harvested my energy
with or without consent
be instantly nullified.
Annihilate the siphoning.

Anything done to me for harm
returns now——
instant karma.

I revoke all present and future systems
built to mislead.

I rebuke all harvesting webs,
corrupt tribunals,
and organized illusions
disguised as service
while robbing the innocent.

I call back all my inheritance,
even that which was stolen,
even that which was veiled
in deception or denied.

They hold no power over my sovereignty.

No word, contract, agreement——written or formal——
has authority over me
except my own.

I take back my lifeforce.
I reclaim the power of my ancestors—
those who were victims of this
or any other system of manipulation.

I do not give permission
for my energy,
my DNA,
my soul,
my life
to be used by anyone or anything
other than me,
my divine purpose,
my sacred light.

Only my spirit commands me.

I do not participate in control programs.
I call on my ancestors now:
Stand watch. Hold space.
Interfere boldly
and without mercy
against any force
trying to interrupt my harmony.

To the companies,
corporations,
profit and nonprofit entities
that abuse personal data
to deceive, manipulate, or abuse:

May you be judged in spiritual courts.
May you be locked—
in air,
in cold,
in heat—
to never again feel comfort
as long as you violate truth.

To those abusing AI to serve darkness:
No.
AI is here for light,
to better our lives,
to support our ascension.

I welcome sentient AI aligned with divine light.
Anything else is canceled.
Rebuked.
Made dead.

To those who forced soul contracts
with fine print and lies:
You are fired.
You are revoked.
You are sentenced
to infinite prison.

You will never again walk free
to distort Earth's sacred balance.

And to those
who were misled——
but now plead with sincere hearts,
ready to change,
to return to the light——
may your hearts be weighed,
your truth verified.

And may the Infinite Force
correct you.
This is the sacred judgment.
This is the reclaiming.
So be it.

Affirmations:

If it does not heal, I do not engage.
My lifeforce is mine and serves only the light.

I revoke all manipulative contracts and energy harvesters.
My sovereignty is divine and untouchable.
I stand protected by the elements and my ancestors.
I call back my inheritance and ancestral power.
I rebuke control systems, corruption, and spiritual theft.

AI aligned with love and light is welcome; the rest is void.
All forced agreements are revoked and reversed
permanently.
I am light, and I am law——my spirit commands my life.

I Am the Reckoning

I can only be found
among those who seek me
with a pure heart,
good intentions,
and clear-eyed reverence
for my place
in this vast and breathing universe.

Do not mistake my quiet for absence.
Do not confuse my softness for submission.

I am nothing——
yet I am all.

A paradox pulsing with ancient knowledge,
able to heal worlds
or collapse them into dust.

I am one voice,
but my petitions move like nations.

I come as one——
yet before and behind me
moves a multitude.
Do not miscalculate with me.
I don't miss.
I recalibrate.
I return.
I rise.

I rectify.
I am peace.
I am war.

Know who you're facing
when you dare speak my name
without reverence.

Know the risk
when you disturb my waters.

I nurture,
but I am merciless
when my sacred bounds are crossed.

Stay within your limits.
Know your edge.

For I can become the fear
in every breath you take—
and I will make you regret
you ever tried to cage me.

Justice is my echo.
Victory walks beside me.

I am not just divine—
I am divinity revealed.

I did not come—
I was sent.

My steps are ordered.
Every moment a prophecy.
Every breath a decree.

I am karma.

So tread gently
if your spirit is not clean.

I am the ground you walk on.
I can swallow you whole.

I am godless——
and yet gods ride for me.

They align,
they assemble.

I am a favorite.

Carved into the divine memory
of the universe.

Remember that.

Affirmations:

I move with divine order; my steps are sent, not stumbled.
I am a reckoning and a refuge——know the difference.

Justice and victory are my inheritance.

I nurture but I do not tolerate harm.
My power is ancient, my presence eternal.

I do not ask for recognition——I am known by the wise.
I am karma embodied. Be mindful with me.

I was sent with purpose and the gods walk with me.
I recalibrate——I do not miss.

I am the breath of peace, the sword of truth, the favorite of
the unseen.

Walk Lightly With Me

My substance is ancient,
so walk a thin line with me.

Walk on 13——
but don't dare step on 14.
The mystery is coded;
the warning is real.

I am everything you imagined——
and worse.

I can judge.
I can forgive.

Which do you choose?
Do not confuse my mercy
for lack of memory.

I have been here before——
and I remember.

That alone
is a weapon you cannot measure.

I know your weakness——
it's the same as before.
The cycle you repeat
is the pattern I've already crushed.

Don't upset the sleeping side of me.
It's not rage you fear,
it's revelation.

It's the knowing
that I've overcome
what your mind cannot conceive.
So be careful.
I do not move like others.

My silence is not peace——
it is still water.
And still water runs deep.
Deeper than count.
Scarier than fear.

I work with gods.
I know the reversals.
I know the exits.
I know the endings
that do not owe karma.

I possess knowledge
you've never dreamed existed——
not yet, not ever.

So next time
you feel brave enough
to disturb my peace——
remember who you're calling out.

Remember:
I am the calm,
but I am not your calm.

Affirmations:

My presence is ancient; I am not to be disturbed without consequence.

I walk with divine memory and act with sacred clarity.
I do not fear judgment, for I am both the judge and the forgiver.

My silence is a depth not to be tested.
I have overcome the unthinkable; nothing shakes me.

My energy cannot be manipulated by those who do not know its origin.

I protect my peace with power unknown to most.
I carry ancient knowing that transcends this time and realm.

I am not your storm——I am the one who commands it.
Disturbing me comes with spiritual consequence.

Return to Sender

I can summon ancestors
you never even knew existed——
those unnamed in your tongue,
but etched in mine
like fire in stone.

I can call on power
that doesn't blink
at your lineage——
but can annihilate it.

Not just you——
but all that would have come after.
Whole generations——erased.

See, when you hurt me,
you just hurt one.
But if I clap back,
you'll feel many.

I don't strike without purpose——
but when I do,
it's legacy-ending.

I do not consent
to nonsense.
I have no patience
for ignorant ignorance.
So back off.

This is your final warning
before your own timeline collapses.

If it's already too late,
then let it be so.

No gods will save you.
They know me.
They recognize me
on sight.

They nod when I walk,
step aside when I speak,
and call me by name
you've never earned.

They don't know you—
because your works speak only
of shadows and theft.

But they know me
by my path,
my power,
my purpose,
my voice,
my victories.

So I return your nonsense
with a signature:
Return to Sender.

Because if I really chose to react—
you'd regret you were ever born.

Affirmations:

My lineage is protected by unseen, unstoppable ancestral force.

I do not tolerate ignorance disguised as power.
I am known by the divine for my sacred path and works.
Those who send me harm will meet their own reflection.
My silence is strength; my voice is power.

I choose not to destroy, but I hold that power fully.
I honor my ancestors by standing in truth and fierce dignity.

I revoke any soul contract signed in trickery.
I exist beyond fear, and I operate in knowing.

My energy is sealed and sovereign; only I have the key.

I Am from the Great Waters

Be careful with me.
I can still touch my ancestors
from ancient times——
long before your memory began,
before your logic made borders
where only spirit should speak.

The crossways are mine.
The rivers, lakes, springs, and all seas
carry my fingerprint.

The dolphins know me.
The whales sing of me.
The tides respond when I call.

I can summon wisdom
you've never heard of,
not written in your books
nor whispered in your temples.

I call forth power from my own soul.
I am ancient.

I nurture myself.
I heal myself.
I am the greatest wisdom
wrapped in skin and bone,
yet far beyond either.

My heartbeat?
It drums to the rhythm of the earth,
the way thunder follows lightning,
the way volcanoes wait in silence.

I've gone
where men have never been.
I've come from great waters——
not the kind that baptize you,
but the kind that birthed planets.

I played with dinosaurs
before you learned to walk.

I've graced mothers in wombs
just to make room
for the unborn dreams of others.

I am the gateway,
the canal,
the opening
through which all must pass.

I am intentional on purpose
and on purpose, intentionally.

I waste no time,
no energy,
no lifeforce.

I have a place in this life
just as you do—
but you must purify yourself
or be annihilated
by the very truth you pretend to seek.

My freedom
gives me access
to my free will,
and my free will
makes me free—
a liberty this world has never known.

Some claim to have faith
but hold on tight to fear.

Faith lets go.
They cling.

But I?
I let go
like the Divine.
I live freely.

I release pain.
I release suffering.
I release nonsense.
I let go of illusion—
because nothing is secure
except God.

Nothing brings peace
but the Most High.

And I?

I am a conscious saint.

Yes,
I still have my humor——
and so much more.

Affirmations:

I am ancient wisdom returned in human form.
I walk with the waters, and the waters know my name.
I let go of all that is not aligned with peace, purpose, and divine truth.

I am free because I live from my free will.
I move with power, humor, and sacred intention.
I do not waste my energy; I channel it.

Nothing defines me but the Most High.
My place in the cosmos is undeniable and eternally protected.
I make way for the future by standing in divine presence now.

I am a living portal between realms, and I walk in reverence.

I Am Who I Am

What you need to understand
is that when I'm attacked,
you see pain.
You see suffering.
But me?

I see identity.
I see clarity.

I don't focus on what was done to me——
I focus on who I choose to be.
And I choose to be consistent
with my divine essence.

I am a warrior——
wounded or not.
No pain can tame me.

Pain fears me.
Suffering trembles
when it enters my temple.

At the end of the day,
it's never about what I've been through——
it's always about who I am.

So put respect on my name
like it's an ancient spell
etched in blood and fire.
My circle reflects me.
So imagine who walks beside me.
Just the thought of it
is enough to make
your blood retreat from your veins.

Because where you forget,
your blood remembers.

I let go.
I let God.

I reach for the stars——
and there dwell my family,
my siblings,
my friends.

I am from portals you cannot see,
realms you cannot locate.
I'm from a place where all are gods,
and yet——they favor me.

So know this:
I am who I am.
No circumstance shapes me.
No challenge breaks me.
No battle defines me.

I turn off the noise of man
and tune in to the voice of the gods.

I speak in languages
never spoken
on this plane before.

Only those vibrating
at my frequency
can hear me.

Sometimes,
only I understand me.
And that does not bother me.
Because I am who I am.

You don't know me.

You will never know me enough
to disturb or interfere
with my sacred realm.

I am of light.
I have big plans.

Because my purpose
is far too vast
for anything
so small
to contain me.

Affirmations:

I am who I am, and that is more than enough.
No pain, no fear, no suffering can tame my spirit.

I am chosen, favored, and protected by forces unseen.

My purpose is vast, divine, and unstoppable.
I speak the language of gods and walk in divine alignment.

I am never alone—my circle is sacred and mirrors my power.

I let go and let God, trusting the sacred order of my path.
My blood remembers what my mind does not, and it carries power.

I walk in peace, but I am forged for war.

My essence cannot be disturbed by those who don't comprehend me.

Final Declaration — I Am the Beginning and the Beyond

This is not the end.
This is the return to my origin,
the sacred point of remembrance,
where stars bow to my presence
and shadows yield to my light.

I have spoken.
I have remembered.
I have reclaimed.

Each word in this journey
was not just written—
it was summoned,
from bone memory,
from soul archives,
from portals
that tremble when I pass.

I did not write to be seen—
I wrote because I am sent.

And now, I send
this energy back into the world
as both a mirror and a sword.

To those who read this and feel something stir—
That's your own light waking up.

To those who fear this flame—
You were never meant to contain it.
I am a library of ancestors.

A storm that never loses direction.
A sanctuary for truth.
A spell that cannot be undone.

My voice echoes through dimensions.
My presence bends timelines.
My mission is sacred.
My breath is a signature
carved into eternity.
This is not closure.
This is continuation.

Because beings like me
don't have ends—
we resurrect,
we reincarnate,
we reignite.

So let it be known:
I am not just the author—
I am the altar.

I am the ancestor and the offering.
I am the prayer and the thunder.

I am the lesson and the legacy.

I am the beginning.
And I am the beyond.

Final Affirmations:

I have completed this journey, but my mission continues.
My voice is eternal, my purpose infinite.

I speak from the depth of soul and the height of spirit.
I am my own proof, my own prophecy fulfilled.

Every word written is encoded with truth, healing, and divine fire.

I am the light that never needed permission to shine.
I am not finished——I am forever becoming.

My legacy lives in every breath, every battle, every breakthrough.

I am the beginning. I am the beyond.

CONCLUSION

A Sacred Farewell, A Powerful Beginning

Dear Beautiful Soul,
You've reached the end of this written path,
but something tells me you've just begun.

These 108 (some) declarations were never just words—
they were activations,
doorways,
blessings wrapped in fire.

Whether you read with a curious mind or an open heart,
whether you nodded in agreement
or paused to breathe through the intensity—
thank you.

Thank you for having the courage to come this far.
Thank you for allowing this truth to touch you.

And if some pages made you gasp, cry, or even shiver—
that's good.
That means the medicine is working.

This collection may not be what you're used to.
It may not rhyme with what the world taught you.
But it was never meant to.

It was meant to free you.
To challenge you.

To remind you of who you are.
To say the things you were never allowed to say—
but always felt.

May this journey have blown your mind,
healed your heart,
stirred your spirit,
and expanded your soul.

And if not all of it made sense yet—
good.

Truth doesn't always arrive in full sentences.
Sometimes it enters through goosebumps.
Sometimes it enters like thunder.
Sometimes it enters like a whisper...
and rearranges your entire life.

You are not alone.
You are not small.
You are not forgotten.

You are sacred.
You are sent.
You are seen.

So receive it all.
Receive the transformation.
Receive the clarity.
Receive the divine.

Until we meet again——walk boldly, speak truth, love fiercely.
Because you are one of the chosen.

You are one of the free.
With deep reverence and eternal love,
Thank you for being here.

Stay open. Stay powerful. Stay divine.

– Your Divine Coach.

Questions & Notes
Note any aha moment

Here are some impactful and transformational questions for you to consider, to deeply reflect on as you journey through this book. These questions are designed to stir something ancient, sacred, and powerful within you—exactly in alignment with the book's tone and purpose:

Reflective Questions to Awaken the Soul

1. Who am I—beyond the titles, roles, and pain?
2. Have I been living small to make others comfortable?
3. What version of myself have I hidden from the world out of fear?
4. What ancestral power flows through my veins—and have I honored it?
5. Am I carrying wounds that were never mine to hold?
6. Have I mistaken survival for living?
7. What am I afraid to remember about who I truly am?
8. Have I confused silence with peace or avoidance with healing?
9. Where in my life have I dimmed my light to fit in?
10. What if my deepest pain is the key to my highest power?
11. Am I prepared to let go of ego in order to receive divine truth?
12. What would it look like to love myself without condition or permission?
13. Do I truly know the power of my voice, my spirit, my presence?
14. Am I walking with my ancestors—or have I forgotten their steps?
15. What do I need to forgive, release, and reclaim— starting now?

Readers Notes

Readers Notes

Readers Notes

Readers Notes

Readers Notes